e.explore

Plant

London, New York, Melbourne,
Munich, and Delhi

Project Editor Clare Hibbert
Weblink Editors Niki Foreman, Phil Hunt

Senior Editor Claire Nottage
Managing Editor Linda Esposito

Digital Development Manager Fergus Day
DTP Co-ordinator Siu Chan

Jacket Copywriter Adam Powley
Jacket Editor Mariza O'Keeffe

Project Art Editor Jane Horne
Illustrators Kuo Kang Chen, Andrew Kerr

Senior Art Editor Jim Green
Managing Art Editor Diane Thistlethwaite

Picture Research Liz Moore
Picture Librarian Claire Bowers

Production Erica Rosen
Jacket Designer Neal Cobourne

Publishing Managers Andrew Macintyre, Caroline Buckingham

Consultant Dr Phil Gates, Senior Lecturer in Botany,
School of Biological and Biomedical Sciences, Durham University

First published in Great Britain in 2006
by Dorling Kindersley Limited, 80 Strand, London WC2R 0RL

Penguin Group

Copyright © 2006 Dorling Kindersley Limited

Google™ is a trademark of Google Technology Inc.

2 4 6 8 10 9 7 5 3 1

A CIP catalogue for this book is available from the British Library.

ISBN-13: 978-1-40531-331-5
ISBN-10: 1-4053-1331-5

Colour reproduction by Colourscan, Singapore
Printed in China by Toppan Printing Co. (Shenzen) Ltd.

Discover more at
www.dk.com

e.explore

Plant

Written by **David Burnie**

Google

CONTENTS

How to use the e.explore website

e.explore Plant has its own website, created by DK and Google™. When you look up a subject in the book, the article gives you key facts and displays a keyword that links you to extra information online. Just follow these easy steps.

http://www.plant.dke-explore.com

 **1** Enter this website address…

Address : @ http://www.plant.dke-explore.com

 **2** Find the keyword in the book…

leaves

 **3** Enter the keyword…

leaves

You can use only the keywords from the book to search on our website for the specially selected DK/Google links.

Be safe while you are online:

- Always get permission from an adult before connecting to the internet.

- Never give out personal information about yourself.

- Never arrange to meet someone you have talked to online.

- If a site asks you to log in with your name or email address, ask permission from an adult first.

- Do not reply to emails from strangers – tell an adult.

Parents: Dorling Kindersley actively and regularly reviews and updates the links. However, content may change. Dorling Kindersley is not responsible for any site but its own. We recommend that children are supervised while online, that they do not use Chat Rooms, and that filtering software is used to block unsuitable material.

4 Click on your chosen link...

5 Download fantastic pictures...

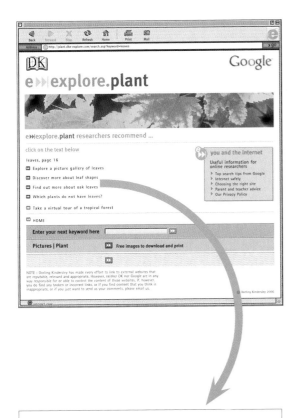

sunflower

The pictures are free of charge, but can be used for personal, non-commercial use only.

▶▶ Discover more about leaf shapes

Links include animations, videos, sound buttons, virtual tours, interactive quizzes, databases, timelines, and realtime reports.

Go back to the book for your next subject...

THE PLANT WORLD

There are more than 400,000 types of plant, and they include the tallest, heaviest, and oldest living things on Earth. Together, they make up the plant kingdom, one of the five kingdoms of living things. Like animals, plants need energy to survive and to grow, but they get it from sunlight instead of from food. Life on Earth depends on plants. All animals eat plants or plant-eaters. As a by-product of making their own food, plants release oxygen – the gas that all animals need to breathe.

◄ THE GREEN PLANET
Plants grow almost everywhere on Earth, and can even be seen from space. Near the equator, conditions for plants are almost perfect, because it is sunny, warm, and wet all year round. This part of the world is home to tropical rainforests, the richest stores of plant life on Earth. Farther away from the equator, life is tougher, and plants must adapt to drought or cold.

Antarctica is home to many kinds of seedless plant but just two kinds of flowering plant

Rainforest plants grow nonstop throughout the year

SEASONS AND PLANTS ►
In temperate parts of the world, such as northern Europe, plants keep in step with the seasons. They start growing in spring, when the days lengthen and the ground begins to warm up. They keep growing in summer but when autumn arrives, their growth stops, and many trees lose their leaves. Winter is a time of rest because the days are short and the ground is often frozen. In warm parts of the world, there is no winter, but the year is often divided into a wet season and a dry season. Plants grow when it is wet, and stop growing when it is dry.

SPRING   SUMMER

AUTUMN   WINTER

THE EVOLUTION OF PLANTS ►
This timeline shows when major plant groups first appeared. It is based on fossil evidence and on molecular clocks (a way of measuring time that uses changes in proteins and genes). The plants shown in the timeline did not evolve from one another. Some, such as liverworts, have existed continuously, unchanged, and have been dead ends. Others evolved more recently from ancient ancestors that are now extinct.

FIRST LAND PLANTS
510 MILLION YEARS AGO (MYA)

LIVERWORTS
475 MYA

MOSSES
450 MYA

HORSETAILS
360 MYA

CLASSIFYING PLANTS ►

Every plant species has its own, two-part scientific name. For example, the early purple orchid is called *Orchis mascula*. The first part gives the plant's genus (*Orchis*). The second part is unique to that species. Scientists classify plants to show how they are all linked by evolution. They split the plant kingdom into smaller groups, such as orders, families, genera, and species.

plant world

Orchis canariensis
Orchis clandestina
Orchis coriophora
Orchis italica
Orchis lactea
Orchis laxiflora
Orchis mascula
Orchis militaris
Orchis morio
Orchis papilionacea
Orchis provincialis
Orchis purpurea
Orchis quadripunctata
Orchis saccata
Orchis sancta
Orchis simia
Orchis spitzelii
Orchis tridentata

MAJOR FAMILIES OF FLOWERING PLANTS

DAISY FAMILY (25,000 SPECIES)
There are more than 300 families of flowering plants, and the daisy family is one of the largest. Plants in this family all produce compound flowers – flower heads made up of lots of miniature flowers, or florets. The daisy family includes many cultivated plants, such as sunflowers and rudbeckias, and also many weeds.

ORCHID FAMILY (25,000 SPECIES)
Orchids grow some of the world's most eye-catching and elaborate flowers. They have tiny seeds, and they depend on fungi to help them germinate and grow. Many orchids grow on the ground, but in warm parts of the world, they are often epiphytic, which means that they perch on other plants. Many orchids store food in swollen roots.

PEA FAMILY (17,000 SPECIES)
This family includes many kinds of trees and shrubs, as well as peas, beans, and other crops. Pea family plants often grow their seeds in pods, and their roots contain nitrogen-fixing bacteria, which help to fertilize the soil. The family contains many ornamental plants, such as lupins and brooms, which are grown for their flowers.

GRASS FAMILY (9,000 SPECIES)
Grasses are the world's most widespread flowering plants. They have tube-like stems, narrow leaves, and feathery, wind-pollinated flowers. Most are low-growing, but bamboos can be over 40 m (130 ft) high. Cultivated grasses include cereals, which are grown for their grain, and sugar cane, which produces sugary sap.

SPURGE FAMILY (5,000 SPECIES)
Spurges grow worldwide, but they are most common in the tropics and in places where the climate is dry. Their flowers are often green and cup-shaped, and their leaves and stems may contain poisonous latex – a fluid that looks like white sap. Latex from one spurge, the rubber tree, is collected and made into natural rubber.

RECORD-BREAKING PLANTS

Tallest living plant	Coast redwood (*Sequoia sempervirens*)	111 m (364 ft)
Heaviest living plant	Giant sequoia (*Sequoiandendron giganteum*)	2,500 tonnes (2,460 tons)
Smallest flowering plant	Australian duckweed (*Wolffia angusta*)	0.6 mm ($\frac{1}{50}$ in) long
Oldest individual plant	Bristlecone pine (*Pinus longaeva*)	5,500 years
Oldest plant clump	Creosote bush (*Larrea tridentata*)	10,000 years
Fastest growing plant	Giant bamboo (*Dendrocalamus giganteus*)	90 cm (3 ft) per day
Largest flower	Rafflesia (*Rafflesia arnoldii*)	90 cm (3 ft) across
Largest leaf	Raffia palm (*Raphia farinifera*)	24 m (79 ft)
Largest fruit (wild)	Jackfruit (*Artocarpus heterophyllus*)	35 kg (77 lb)
Largest fruit (cultivated)	Pumpkin (*Cucurbita pepo*)	606 kg (1,337 lb)
Deepest roots	Wild fig (*Ficus palmata*)	120 m (400 ft)

FERNS
360 MYA

CYCADS
290 MYA

GINKGOS
290 MYA

CONIFERS
290 MYA

FLOWERING PLANTS
145 MYA

WHAT IS A PLANT?

Most people have no difficulty telling an animal from a plant. That is because animals can move about, while plants are rooted in one spot. But what is it that makes a plant a plant? Like animals, plants are living things that are made up of lots of cells; unlike animals, plants make their own food by photosynthesis (see pages 18–19), a process that harnesses the energy in sunlight. Most plants have roots, stems, and leaves, and most (although not all) reproduce by growing flowers and making seeds. Algae, fungi, and lichens have some plantlike characteristics, but they do not belong to the plant kingdom.

PLANT CELLS ▶

Plants are built from microscopic living units called cells. Each cell has a tough cell wall that is made of cellulose. The wall gives the cell its shape. The cell contains fluid under pressure, which presses out against the cell wall and keeps the cell firm. Plants have many kinds of cells. These ones, from a leaf, contain green structures called chloroplasts, which collect energy from sunlight and carry out photosynthesis.

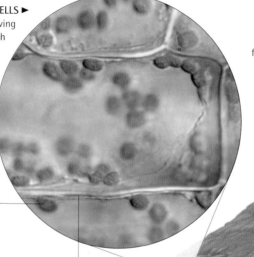

Chloroplast intercepts sunlight shining through the cell

Cell wall is made of overlapping fibres of cellulose

PLANT ANATOMY ▶

This primrose is a typical flowering plant. It is divided into two parts. The first part is the root system, which anchors the plant and also absorbs water and nutrients from the soil. The second part is the shoot system, which includes all the parts above ground, such as the stems, leaves, and flowers. The roots and shoots grow in a balanced way, so that the roots are able to deliver all the water that the plant needs.

Water vapour evaporates from the surface of the leaf

PLANT REPRODUCTION

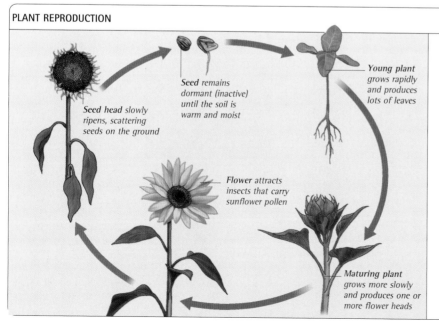

Seed head slowly ripens, scattering seeds on the ground

Seed remains dormant (inactive) until the soil is warm and moist

Young plant grows rapidly and produces lots of leaves

Flower attracts insects that carry sunflower pollen

Maturing plant grows more slowly and produces one or more flower heads

Many plants reproduce in two different ways. The first method, sexual reproduction, involves male and female cells. In flowering plants, such as sunflowers, the male cells are inside pollen grains. The female cells, or ova, are fertilized by the pollen, and develop into seeds.

When the seeds are ripe, they are scattered by the parent plant. They start to grow, or germinate, when conditions are right. Each one develops into a new plant, which produces its own seeds, and the cycle begins again.

Plants can also reproduce without using sex cells. This is called asexual reproduction. It happens when a plant grows special parts that turn into new plants.

plant world

Leaf collects energy from sunlight

SIMPLE PLANTS ▶
The first land plants were very simple, without roots, stems, leaves, or flowers. The plant world has changed since then, but simple plants still exist. The most common kinds are mosses and liverworts, like the ones growing around this stream. These plants absorb water through their outer surface. Most of them live in places that are shady and damp.

Stem supports flowers or leaves and carries water and nutrients up from the roots

Colourful flower attracts pollinating animals

SINGLE-CELLED GREEN ALGA

SEAWEED

FUNGUS

LICHEN

Node is where leaf attaches to stem

▲ PLANT LOOKALIKES
Seaweeds and other algae live in a similar way to plants, because their cells contain chloroplasts that gather the energy in sunlight. Algae and plants share distant ancestors, but they belong to separate kingdoms. Fungi make up another kingdom. They can look like plants, but their cells are built very differently. They do not need light, and get their energy by digesting living things or dead remains. Lichens are not plants, either. They are permanent partnerships between fungi and microscopic algae.

SPECIALIZED PLANTS

Taproot stores food and anchors the plant

Lateral root spreads out to collect water and nutrients

XEROPHYTE
Plants that have adapted to life in dry places are called xerophytes. This living baseball plant is a xerophyte. It has deep roots that search out moisture, and fleshy stems that store water and keep the plant alive in a drought. Many xerophytes lack leaves – their stems collect the sunlight that they need to grow.

HALOPHYTE
Sea heath is a widespread halophyte, or salt-tolerant plant. It grows close to the sea and can survive being soaked by salty spray. Halophytes also grow inland, for example in salt marshes or next to salt lakes. Road verges are another halophyte habitat, because there is a build-up of salt that has been used to thaw ice.

HYDROPHYTE
Plants that live in water, such as this lotus, are called hydrophytes. Plants are very common in freshwater, such as ponds and rivers. Some root on the bottom, while others float in the water or on the surface. Far fewer plants live in sea water. Instead, the oceans are home to plantlike seaweeds and other algae.

STEMS AND ROOTS

A plant's stem holds it upright and connects its roots with its leaves. It contains bundles of microscopic pipelines that carry water, minerals, and food. Some plant stems are slimmer than a pencil and bend in the breeze. Others may be over 3 m (10 ft) thick. Roots carry out two tasks: they anchor the plant and they absorb water and minerals from the soil. In some plants, particularly ones that live in dry places, the roots can be bigger than all the parts above ground.

Terminal bud enables the stem to lengthen

Node can bear a single leaf, or several

Leaf vein connects with xylem and phloem vessels in the stem

ANATOMY OF A STEM ▶
The inside of a plant stem contains xylem and phloem vessels – microscopic pipelines that carry water, minerals, and food. The outside is covered with epidermal cells, which protect the stem from damage and stop it drying out. The stem grows longer at its terminal bud, which contains rapidly dividing cells. Further down the stem, leaves are attached at points called nodes.

stems and roots

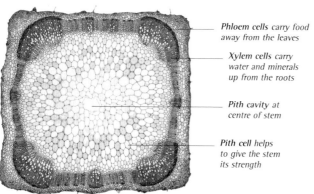

Phloem cells carry food away from the leaves

Xylem cells carry water and minerals up from the roots

Pith cavity at centre of stem

Pith cell helps to give the stem its strength

DEAD-NETTLE STEM

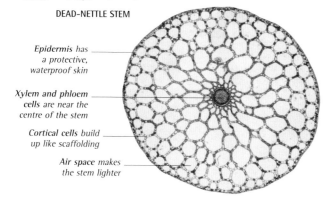

Epidermis has a protective, waterproof skin

Xylem and phloem cells are near the centre of the stem

Cortical cells build up like scaffolding

Air space makes the stem lighter

MARE'S-TAIL STEM

▲ INSIDE STEMS
These two stems have been sliced in half to show how they are built. The dead-nettle's stem is square, with bundles of xylem and phloem cells arranged near the outside. The mare's-tail stem is round, with xylem and phloem cells close to the centre. Both stems have air spaces, which help them to be light as well as strong, and both are herbaceous, which means that they die down to the ground in the winter.

◀ GROWING TALLER
After pushing up through the soil, this giant bamboo stem is beginning its journey up towards the light. Like all stems, it grows because its cells divide. In many plants, including bamboo, the growth occurs at the tip of the stem. Further down, the stem stops growing after it has formed. Bamboos include the world's fastest growing plants. Some shoot up a further 90 cm (3 ft) each day – almost fast enough to see with the naked eye.

◀ GROWING THICKER
As well as growing taller, some stems thicken. This thickening, or secondary growth, occurs in the stems and branches of all woody plants, including this beech tree. Beneath their bark, woody plants have two thin sheets of rapidly dividing cells. The inner sheet produces new wood, while the outer one produces new bark. This means that trunks and branches grow thicker and stronger each year, and also that woody plants can repair minor wounds.

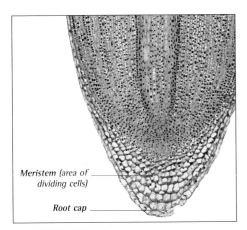

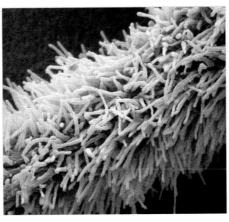

▲ HOW ROOTS GROW

This photograph shows the root tip of a lily, magnified over 100 times. Like stems, roots grow at their tips where there is an area of cells that are dividing. The tip of the root is covered by a cap, which protects the dividing cells. The cap has an outer layer of slime, which helps the growing root to slip between particles of soil. Root tips respond to the force of gravity by growing downwards – the best direction for finding water in the soil.

Meristem (area of dividing cells)

Root cap

▲ ROOT HAIRS

Behind its tip, each root sprouts a forest of extremely fine hairs, like the ones in this micrograph of a marjoram plant. Root hairs reach into the soil and absorb water and nutrients. Although root hairs are small, plants have huge numbers of them. For example, a single rye plant has more than 10,000 km (6,200 miles) of root hairs, measured end to end. When plants are moved, they have to be dug up very gently, so that their root hairs are not destroyed.

▲ SPECIALIZED ROOTS

Many plants use their roots for storing food. Root crops such as beetroots, carrots, turnips, and swedes are natural food stores. One root crop, sugar beet, is packed with sweet sap, which can be boiled down to make sugar. In swampy places, some trees have special breathing roots, which grow up from the mud. Some climbing plants grow specialized roots, too. Ivy uses its roots to grip solid objects as it grows up towards the light.

ROOT SYSTEMS ►

A young apple tree has spreading roots, which grow near the surface. This kind of root system keeps the tree well-anchored, even when its branches are tugged by gale-force winds. A dandelion's root system is quite different. It has a deep taproot, with only a few small side roots leading off it. This kind of root system is good for storing food and water, and it also makes the plant very difficult to dig up.

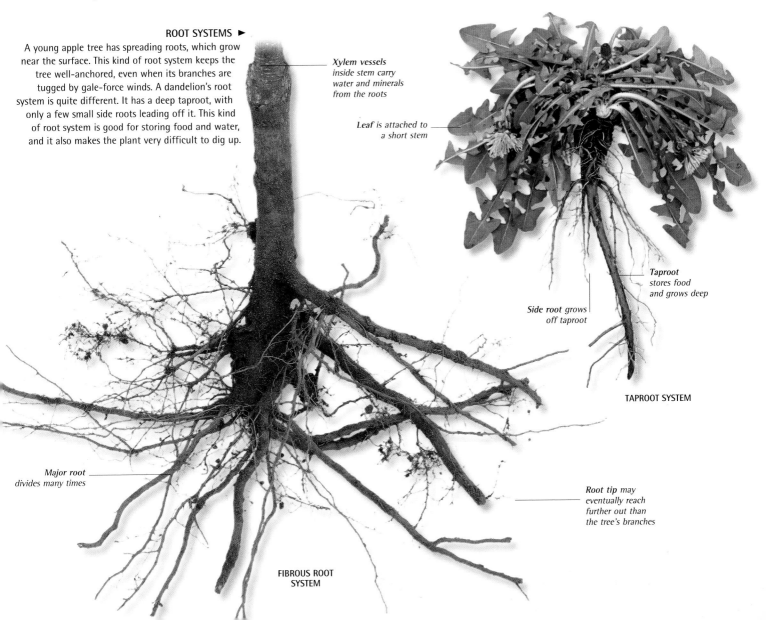

Xylem vessels inside stem carry water and minerals from the roots

Leaf is attached to a short stem

Taproot stores food and grows deep

Side root grows off taproot

TAPROOT SYSTEM

Major root divides many times

Root tip may eventually reach further out than the tree's branches

FIBROUS ROOT SYSTEM

TRANSPIRATION

From the moment they start to grow, plants soak up water through their roots, and lose it from their leaves. The process of water evaporating into the air is called transpiration. A small seedling transpires just a few drops of water a week, but a fully grown tree can transpire over 1,000 litres (265 gallons) in a single day. During transpiration, water evaporates from leaves through microscopic pores called stomata. These pores can open and close to control the flow of water vapour. Transpiration is vital for plants. The act of losing water creates a suction force that helps plants to collect essential minerals and nutrients from the soil.

Flower also loses water through transpiration

HOW TRANSPIRATION WORKS ▶
Like all flowering plants, a daisy moves water by a combination of pushing and pulling. The push comes from the roots, which pump water a little way up the stem. The pull comes when water evaporates from its leaves, because this draws more water up the plant to take its place. Water travels up the plant in xylem cells, which work like microscopic pipelines. Xylem cells run from the tips of the plant's roots to the pores, or stomata, in its leaves.

▼ WATER ON THE MOVE
In the steamy heat of the tropics, rainforests transpire enormous amounts of water vapour. This moisture determines the local weather, because it helps to produce clouds that soak the forest with rain. Plants transpire even more quickly in hot and dry conditions, which is why desert plants need special features to stop themselves drying out. Transpiration is slowest in places where the air is cold, and where there is little wind.

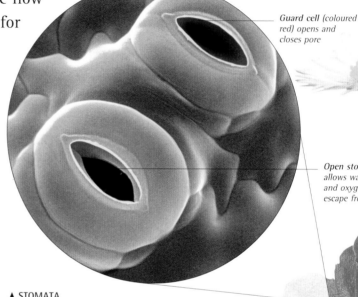

Guard cell (coloured red) opens and closes pore

Open stoma (pore) allows water vapour and oxygen to escape from leaf

▲ STOMATA
When water reaches a plant's leaves, most of it evaporates through tiny holes or pores called stomata. Each stoma is bordered by two guard cells, which can change shape to make the pore open or close. The pore leads into a network of air spaces hidden inside the leaf. Here, leaf cells take up carbon dioxide – a gas that plants need in order to grow – from the air. At the same time, the cells give up water vapour and oxygen. These escape through the pore and into the air outside.

Packing cells surround the pipelines

Spiral thickenings on cell wall

WATER PIPELINES ▶
When water travels through a plant, it moves along pipelines formed by xylem cells. Each narrower than a hair, the pipelines help the water molecules to stick together in long columns. The xylem cells have reinforced walls so that they do not collapse as their water is sucked upwards. In warm, sunny weather, water can travel 40 m (130 ft) in an hour.

Stoma allows water vapour to escape at night

Waxy coating stops water evaporating through leaf surface

Air chamber within leaf contains water vapour

Maize leaf has withered and died without water

▲ DROUGHT

After weeks without any rain, these maize plants have shrivelled up and died. Drought is disastrous for plants, because it brings transpiration to a halt. The first signs of trouble are when the leaves droop and the plant starts to wilt. This happens because plant cells need water to stay firm – if they run short, they lose their shape. If the plant gets water soon enough, it can usually recover. If not, its cells start to dry out and the whole plant begins to die.

▲ SAVING WATER

Plants that live in dry places – such as this *Aloe vera* – have to be economical with water. They store water in their roots, stems, or leaves, and they transpire much more slowly than other plants. They have fewer stomata, and instead of opening them during the day, they open them at night. This is because the air is usually much cooler after dark. Water evaporates more slowly when it is cold, so the plants lose less moisture.

Leaf surface has stomata that allow water vapour to escape

WATER PUMP ►

In the early morning, the leaves of low-growing plants are sometimes edged with droplets. This water is not dew. It has come from the plant. This happens on cool, still nights, when a plant's roots force water into the leaves faster than it can evaporate. Instead of escaping into the air, it is squeezed out in drops. This is called guttation.

transpiration

Root pushes water upwards

SAP

Using its syringe-like mouthparts, this aphid (or greenfly) has pierced a plant stem and is sucking up the sap from inside. Sap is often thick and sticky, because it contains the sugary food that plants make in their leaves. Unlike water, it travels in pipelines made of phloem cells, and it can move down a plant as well as up.

Plants use sap to carry food where it is needed. In the spring, sap often takes food from a plant's roots to its leaf buds, so that they can start to grow. In the autumn, food travels down to the roots, so that it can be stored during the winter.

LEAVES

Leaves are like a plant's solar panels. They collect energy from sunlight, so that plants can use it to grow. They also release water vapour and oxygen, and absorb carbon dioxide from the air. Leaves are built from living cells and they have a huge variety of shapes. These have evolved so that leaves can work efficiently in different conditions, without being dried out by strong sunshine or damaged by the wind. Leaves also have varied life spans. Some of them last for years, while others work for just a few months before they wither and die.

Compound leaf with three leaflets that are roughly the same size

leaves

LABURNUM

Central midrib connects to network of smaller veins

SHAPES AND COLOURS ▶
Leaves consist of a flat blade, strengthened by ribs called veins. Simple leaves, such as those grown by the common beech, have a single blade. Compound leaves, such as those grown by laburnums and walnuts, have separate blades called leaflets that are attached to a central stalk. A laburnum leaf has just three leaflets and a black walnut leaf has up to 23, but some compound leaves have over a hundred. Most leaves are green, but some have special pigments that give them a coppery colour. Plants with unusual leaf colours are prized by gardeners.

COMMON BEECH

WALNUT

Compound leaf with leaflets arranged in two rows

WILD BANANA
(LARGE LEAVES)

MOUNTAIN SAXIFRAGE
(SMALL LEAVES)

◀ LEAVES AND CLIMATE
Leaves have evolved to fit all kinds of habitats. The wild banana grows in tropical rainforest. Its large leaves make the most of any sunlight that filters through the tree tops. Large leaves lose more water through evaporation, but rain is plentiful here. At the other extreme, saxifrages have very small leaves. They live on mountains and their leaves have to be able to cope with bright sunshine, gales, and temperatures that fall well below freezing.

ENGLISH OAK: 6 MONTHS

STONE PINE: 3 YEARS

AGAVE: 10 YEARS

WELWITSCHIA: 1,000+ YEARS

▲ LEAF LIFE SPANS

Some leaves are designed to be disposable, while others last for many years. Deciduous trees, such as the English oak, shed their leaves each autumn and then grow a new set the following spring. Evergreen trees keep their leaves all year round. Depending on the tree, each evergreen leaf has a life span between three and 40 years. The world's oldest leaves belong to a desert plant called welwitschia. It has just two leaves and they last for the whole of its life, which can be over 1,000 years.

◄ GIANT LEAVES

The world's biggest leaves are grown by the raffia palm, which grows on islands in the Indian Ocean. Its leaves grow as long as 24 m (79 ft), from the base of the stalk to the tip. The plant is cultivated on plantations because its stalks are the source of raffia, a natural fibre used in handicrafts. The world's largest simple leaves (ones without leaflets) belong to banana plants and their relatives. Banana leaves can be more than 2.5 m (8 ft) long – big enough to use as giant umbrellas during tropical downpours.

MODIFIED LEAVES

Some plants have modified leaves. Cacti collect light with their stems. Over millions of years, their leaves have steadily shrunk and evolved into spines, which protect them from hungry animals. Climbing plants often have thread-like tendrils, which coil around solid supports. Some are modified stems, but most are modified leaves with touch-sensitive tips.

SENSITIVE LEAVES

LEAVES OPEN
Also known as the sensitive plant, mimosa is a low-growing weed that lives in warm parts of the world. Most of the time, its leaves spread out flat to catch as much light as possible. This means the leaves can attract the attention of plant-eating animals, but the sensitive plant has a remarkable way of suddenly vanishing.

LEAVES CLOSED
If a grazing animal touches just one leaflet of a mimosa plant, its stalk closes like a hinge. This movement quickly spreads along the leaf, until all the leaflets have folded up. Now that the leaves are hidden, the animal usually loses interest and moves on. Over the next half hour, the leaflets slowly open out once more.

Finely branching aquatic leaf can cope with water currents

Aerial leaf is round and flat to take in sunlight

TWIN LEAVES ►

Freshwater plants often have two different types of leaf. This water crowfoot plant has rounded leaves that grow above the surface, and finely divided leaves that grow underwater. Each type of leaf is shaped to work in different surroundings. Plants can also have different leaves when they are young and when they are mature. Many eucalyptuses have coin-shaped leaves when they are young (so that they can absorb maximum sunshine for photosynthesis), and narrow leaves when they are adult (in order to minimise how much water they lose).

LIVING ON LIGHT

Unlike animals, plants do not get energy by eating food. Instead, they get it directly from sunlight. They use light to turn carbon dioxide and water into glucose – a sugar that works like a fuel. Glucose powers all the plant's cells and enables them to divide and grow. This way of living is called photosynthesis, which means "putting together with light". Photosynthesis takes place in the plant's leaves, inside tiny structures called chloroplasts. It is vital for plants, and also for animals, because without it there would be no plant food for animals to eat.

Carbon dioxide enters the leaf through its stomata (pores)

Glucose is carried from the leaf to other parts of the plant

PHOTOSYNTHESIS IN ACTION ▶
To photosynthesize, a plant needs just three ingredients – sunlight, carbon dioxide, and water. Carbon dioxide enters the plant's leaves through tiny pores called stomata, and water travels up to the leaves from the soil, through pipelines in the plant's roots and stems. Once carbon dioxide and water are inside a leaf, photosynthesis can start. Photosynthesis produces two substances: glucose, which the plant uses; and oxygen, which flows out of the pores as waste.

Oxygen leaves the leaf through its stomata (pores)

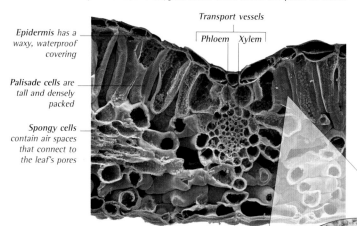

Epidermis has a waxy, waterproof covering

Transport vessels
Phloem   Xylem

Palisade cells are tall and densely packed

Spongy cells contain air spaces that connect to the leaf's pores

◀ INSIDE A LEAF
This cross section through a leaf shows the cells that carry out photosynthesis. Just underneath the leaf's outer skin, or epidermis, are the tall and narrow palisade cells. These are packed with chloroplasts – green structures that trap light and use it for photosynthesis. Beneath the palisade cells are spongy cells that are separated by air spaces. The spaces contain carbon dioxide and water vapour – two of the ingredients that are needed for photosynthesis to work.

CHLOROPLASTS ▶
A plant's chloroplasts intercept sunlight as it shines through its leaves. Using a green pigment called chlorophyll, the chloroplasts trap the energy, and use it to combine the carbon dioxide and water. Each chloroplast contains coin-shaped membranes, called thylakoids, set in a watery fluid called the stroma. Thylakoids are like chemical work surfaces, where light energy splits water molecules apart. In the stroma, hydrogen from water molecules is combined with carbon dioxide to make glucose.

Stroma produces glucose

Stacks of thylakoids (chlorophyll membranes)

Stored food (starch) made by photosynthesis

light

KEY
- Oxygen
- Glucose
- Water
- Carbon dioxide

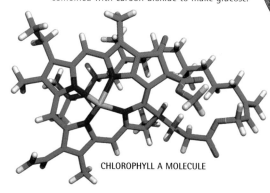

CHLOROPHYLL A MOLECULE

◀ CHLOROPHYLL
A chemical called chlorophyll gives chloroplasts their green colour. Chlorophyll absorbs the energy in sunlight and turns it into chemical energy that a plant can use. There are several kinds of chlorophyll. One of them, called chlorophyll a, is found in all green plants, as well as in algae and cyanobacteria. Using their chlorophyll, these living things collect about 1 per cent of all the light energy that reaches the Earth every year.

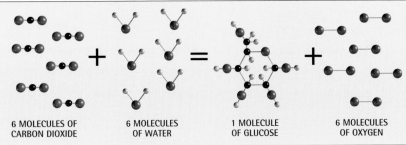

Water evaporates from the leaf

Green light reflects off the chlorophyll in the leaf

Water is pushed and pulled up through the stem

◄ WATER SUPPLIES

To carry out photosynthesis, plants need a constant supply of moisture. In most plants, water is collected by the roots and delivered to the leaves by transpiration. Only a small amount of this water is used in photosynthesis. Most of it evaporates through the plant's pores, and escapes into the air.

Water is absorbed from the soil by the roots

◄ WHY PLANTS ARE GREEN

Sunlight is made up of all the colours of the rainbow. Chlorophyll is good at collecting the energy from the red and orange parts of sunlight, and also from blue and violet. However, it is not nearly so good at collecting green parts of the spectrum. This unused light bounces off leaves or shines through them and it makes them look green. Many plants – such as grasses – are green all over, because they have chlorophyll in their stems as well as in their leaves.

THE CHEMISTRY OF PHOTOSYNTHESIS

6 MOLECULES OF CARBON DIOXIDE + 6 MOLECULES OF WATER = 1 MOLECULE OF GLUCOSE + 6 MOLECULES OF OXYGEN

Photosynthesis is a complicated process that involves many different steps. However, in plants, the overall result is quite simple. Glucose is made from carbon dioxide and water, and oxygen is created as a waste product.

To make one molecule of glucose, a plant needs six molecules of water and six molecules of carbon dioxide. Using energy from sunlight, the water molecules are split apart. The water's hydrogen atoms join up with the carbon dioxide to make one glucose molecule. The water's oxygen atoms escape into the air.

Photosynthesis has created all the oxygen in the atmosphere. It is responsible for all the living plants on Earth's surface, and all the fossil fuels (such as coal and oil) that are buried below ground.

KEY
- carbon atom
- oxygen atom
- hydrogen atom

USING GLUCOSE

 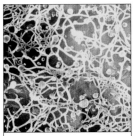 

SUCROSE
Plants use glucose as a first step towards making many other useful substances. One of these is sucrose, the sugar that we use to sweeten food. Sucrose is found in plant sap. It is rich in energy, and is produced commercially from sugar cane or sugar beet. The sap is boiled up to turn the sucrose into sugar crystals.

CELLULOSE
Plants use cellulose to build their cell walls. To make it, they put together long chains or fibres of glucose molecules. These fibres often crisscross together to form layers, which gives them extra strength. Cellulose makes up over a third of every plant, which makes it one of the most common substances in the living world.

STARCH
These balloon-like objects are grains of starch from a potato. Plants use starch to store energy, and they stock it in their leaves, roots, and seeds. Unlike sucrose, starch does not dissolve in water, so it can be left in storage for a long time. Starch supplies most of the energy that we get from plant-based foods.

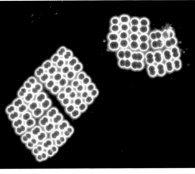

◄ PHOTOSYNTHESIS IN BACTERIA

Plants are not the only things that live by photosynthesis – bacteria do, too. These *Merismopedia* live in freshwater, but photosynthetic bacteria are found in many other habitats, including hot springs and the ocean. Photosynthetic bacteria all contain chlorophyll, but many also have other pigments that make them look blue-green, yellowish, or even purple. Bacteria used photosynthesis long before the first plants appeared. Over millions of years, they released oxygen into the air and created a breathable atmosphere.

HOW PLANTS GROW

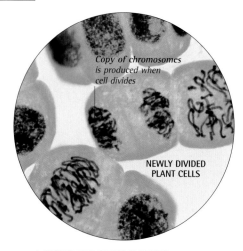

Copy of chromosomes is produced when cell divides

NEWLY DIVIDED PLANT CELLS

▲ GENES AND CHROMOSOMES
Every plant cell contains packages of genes called chromosomes. The cells here have been dyed to make their chromosomes easy to see. Each chromosome holds thousands of separate genes. Together, genes control the way the plant works and how it grows. Plants grow by enlarging their cells, and also by making cells divide in two. Just before a cell divides, its chromosomes copy themselves, so that each new cell receives a complete set of its own.

Most animals grow in a set way, which is programmed by their genes. Even when they are small, it's easy to say what they will look like when they are fully grown. Plants are different. Their growth is controlled by genes too, but their final shape also depends on where they live. For example, a tree can be big and broad if it grows up in the open, but much taller and thinner if it grows in woodland, where there are other trees all around. Plants are unable to move from one environment to another, so it is important that they are able to adapt to their habitat. Chemicals inside plants, called growth regulators, enable them to adjust to the world around them as they grow.

Tall rice plant contains extra growth regulator

Standard-sized plants contain ordinary levels of growth regulator

◄ GROWTH REGULATORS
In the middle of this rice field, one extra-tall plant stands out. It is bigger than the others because it has produced extra gibberellin – one of the substances that plants use to regulate (control) their growth. Growth regulators do not only affect a plant's height. They make its leaves and stems turn towards the light, and they also help it to stay in step with the seasons by triggering growth at the right time.

OAK TREE IN OPEN LANDSCAPE

OAK TREES IN CROWDED WOODLAND

◄ REACHING FOR THE LIGHT
A plant's growth regulators allow it to react to the environment and can affect the plant's shape. When an oak tree grows in the open, there is sunlight all around. Its branches grow outwards in all directions, giving the tree a spreading shape. When oak trees grow in woodland, they are shaded by their neighbours and must compete for light. Their growth regulators make them grow tall and thin, so that they can get the best share of the light.

growing

PRUNING

Farmers and gardeners often prune plants as they grow. After several years of patient pruning, this bush has been turned into an elephant, complete with a rider on its back. Pruning is used to train plants into extraordinary or beautiful shapes, but it can have a useful purpose, too. When shrubs and trees are pruned, they often produce more flowers and fruit. Pruning can also make plants live longer, because their oldest branches are less likely to split and break off.

No twigs have survived onshore winds

SCULPTED BY THE WIND ▲

Near the coast, many trees and shrubs are shaped by the wind. Any twigs that try to grow towards the wind are killed off, but those growing on the other side of the trunk are able to grow. After many years, this produces plants with a lopsided shape, such as this 50-year-old hawthorn, growing in a field. The tree looks as though it is about to topple over, but its uneven shape actually helps it to survive.

METHODS OF SURVIVAL

▲ TALL OR SMALL
Soil affects how plants grow. These common poppies are in a cornfield, where the soil is rich and moist. They have grown as high as the corn because their roots are in fertile soil. In poor, dry ground, the same kind of poppies grow to only about 8 cm (3 in) high. They still flower, but produce fewer seeds.

▲ MOUNTAIN MINIATURES
This stunted pine tree is growing from a crevice in solid rock on a mountainside. It must cope with cold winds and little water, because any rain soon runs off bare rock. Amazingly, trees do survive in such conditions. Some even live close to the snow line, where their trunks snake their way across the ground.

▲ KEEPING A LOW PROFILE
A limestone pavement is a strange, rocky landscape that has hardly any soil. From a distance, the blocks of limestone look bare and barren, but many different plants grow in the deep, natural cracks. These cracks, called grikes, hide the plants from hungry animals and shelter them from the wind.

▲ SURVIVING ACCIDENTS
Several weeks after a bushfire, this eucalyptus tree sprouts new leaves. Special buds all over the trunk start to grow if the existing branches die. If the whole tree is burned, the plant regrows from the ground. Although plants cannot run away from trouble, many survive disaster by growing back once it has passed.

PLANT LIFE SPANS

Plants have an amazing range of life spans. Some rush through life in a few weeks, while others survive for thousands of years. The oldest plants alive today started life before the first pyramids were built, and when the wheel was still a new invention. Over the course of their lives – short or long – plants divide up their time in different ways. Many put all their energy into a single burst of reproduction, flowering and setting seed just once in a lifetime. Others play a waiting game. Instead of breeding in a one-off burst, they keep flowering year after year.

life spans

▲ ANNUAL PLANTS
Garden marigolds are annual plants, which means that they grow, flower, and die in less than a year. After flowering, they concentrate on making seeds. Annuals include many colourful garden plants and also many weeds. Annuals often spring up on wasteland, where the soil has been exposed. They set seed as fast as they can, before longer-lived plants move in.

▲ BIENNIAL PLANTS
This mullein plant lives for two years. During its first year, it builds up its leaves and food reserves. During its second year, it uses up its food stores to make flowers and seeds. After it has set seed, it dies. Plants like this are called biennials. They are not as common as annuals, but they include some eye-catching plants, such as mulleins and foxgloves.

▲ PERENNIAL PLANTS
Plants that live for many years are called perennials. Roses are typical examples: in gardens, some kinds have been known to live for over a century. Perennials include all the world's trees and shrubs, as well as herbaceous plants, which die back in autumn, then sprout again in spring. Most perennials flower every year, but a few flower just once and then die.

SHEPHERD'S PURSE: 4 MONTHS

MULLEIN: 2 YEARS

▼ SHORT AND LONG LIVES
This chart shows typical life spans for six very different plants. Shepherd's purse is a short-lived annual that speeds through its existence in just four months. Mulleins nearly always survive for two years, while rockroses (not related to ordinary roses) typically survive for 10 years. Many bamboos have set life spans, which can be up to 120 years long. At the end of this time, a bamboo clump flowers and dies. Baobabs often live for over a thousand years, but bristlecone pines take the record for the longest-lived individual plants – at least 4,600 years.

ROCKROSE: 10 YEARS

BAMBOO: 120 YEARS

BAOBAB: 1,000 YEARS

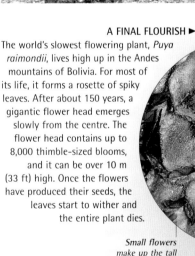

◄ EPHEMERAL PLANTS

Desert flowers called ephemerals have some of the shortest life spans in the plant world. Instead of blooming at a particular time of year, their seeds lie dormant (inactive) until it rains. After a downpour, the seeds germinate (sprout), grow into plants, and flower in record time. By the time the earth dries out again, the ephemerals have finished their life cycle and their seeds have been scattered across the desert ground.

Huge flower head towers above the leaves

◄ ANCIENT TREES

With its bare wood and twisted branches, this bristlecone pine looks nearly dead, but these trees are amazing survivors. Some live to be more than 4,600 years old, and even this gnarled specimen could last another 500 years. Found on dry, cold mountainsides in the western USA, bristlecone pines grow less than 2 cm (¾ in) a year. Their tiny leaves are able to withstand the drying effect of the wind in their exposed, high-altitude home.

▲ KEEPING IN STEP

In temperate parts of the world, where there are clear-cut seasons, plants must flower at the right time of year. Daffodils start growing in late winter, from bulbs buried in the ground. Their leaves push through the surface in early spring, and by early summer they have finished flowering and set seed. Plants keep in step with the seasons by monitoring conditions such as soil temperature, rainfall, and the number of hours of daylight.

A FINAL FLOURISH ►

The world's slowest flowering plant, *Puya raimondii*, lives high up in the Andes mountains of Bolivia. For most of its life, it forms a rosette of spiky leaves. After about 150 years, a gigantic flower head emerges slowly from the centre. The flower head contains up to 8,000 thimble-sized blooms, and it can be over 10 m (33 ft) high. Once the flowers have produced their seeds, the leaves start to wither and the entire plant dies.

Small flowers make up the tall flower head

▲ CREOSOTE BUSH CLONES

The world's oldest plants are not individuals, but connected clumps called clones. Clones of creosote bush live for more than 10,000 years – longer than any other living thing. Creosote bush grows in the deserts of the western USA. The clumps may form rings around the place where one seed took root long ago. Bracken forms clones, too, and can live for over 2,000 years.

Leaves store up food so plant can flower

BRISTLECONE PINE: 4,600 YEARS

Spiky leaves discourage plant-eating animals

BROWN
SEAWEED

GREEN
SEAWEED

RED
SEAWEED

ALGAE

Algae existed on Earth long before the first true plants. Today, they still flourish wherever there is water and sunlight. Most kinds of algae live in the sea or in freshwater, but some grow in damp places on land. Unlike plants, algae do not have true roots, stems, or leaves. The smallest have just a single cell, and often spend their lives adrift. The largest kinds are brown seaweeds called kelps. They look more like plants, and can grow longer than 50 m (164 ft). Algae are very important for animals as food, and some animals also benefit by living with algae as partners.

◄ SEAWEEDS

Like true plants, seaweeds contain green chlorophyll, but many contain other pigments that make them look brown or red. Green seaweeds often live in brackish (slightly salty) water, brown seaweeds are common in shallow water close to the shore, and red seaweeds usually live in deeper water, beyond the reach of the waves. All seaweeds have leafy fronds, and a root-like anchor called a holdfast.

Spiral chloroplast collects energy from sunlight

algae

Egg cell is formed by sexual reproduction

PHYTOPLANKTON

This colour-enhanced satellite map shows the amount of chlorophyll on Earth. Chlorophyll is produced by plants on land and by phytoplankton and seaweeds in the oceans. Phytoplankton are microscopic algae that drift near the surface of the water. They are so numerous that together they weigh more than all the plants on land. Phytoplankton make up a huge reserve of food for sea animals, from fish to giant baleen whales (toothless whales such as blue, humpback, and right whales).

Algae grow best in cooler water that is rich in dissolved nutrients. On this satellite map, the green and light blue areas of the oceans contain the most phytoplankton and the dark blue areas contain the least. The black and red areas are where the satellite was unable to pick up any data. Most phytoplankton are in the far north and south. These regions teem with animal life.

CHLOROPHYLL DENSITY

IN THE OCEAN
- High
- Medium
- Low

ON LAND
- High
- Medium
- Low

▲ LIVING IN COLONIES

This green slime is an alga called *Spirogyra*, which thrives in stagnant water and is found in ditches and shallow ponds. *Spirogyra* produces a mass of filaments, each thinner than a human hair. Each filament is an algal colony – a collection of identical cells that live together. Individual *Spirogyra* cells are long and thin, with spiral chloroplasts (particles containing chlorophyll) that stretch from one end of the cell to the other.

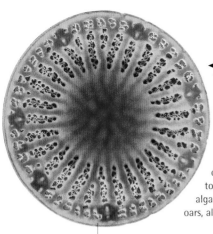

◄ SINGLE-CELLED ALGAE

This beautiful object is a diatom, a single-celled alga that lives inside an intricate case. The case is built of silica, the same hard substance used to make glass. Single-celled algae live in the oceans, in freshwater, and in many other damp habitats, including the top of the soil. Some single-celled algae have tiny hairs that work like oars, allowing them to swim.

Half diatom case
fits over other half
like the lid of a box

Daughter colonies
are made by asexual
reproduction

Clam's lips
retract before
shell closes

LIVE-IN PARTNERS ►

Holding its massive shell open, this giant clam exposes its brightly coloured lips. They get their colour from microscopic algae that live inside the clam's cells. The clam gives the algae a safe place to live and, in return, it gets some of the food that the algae make. Many other animals use algae as live-in partners. They range from tiny flatworms to corals that build reefs.

HOW ALGAE REPRODUCE ▲

Swimming through the water of a pond, these ball-shaped algae called *Volvox* are carrying their young aboard. The parents will eventually break open, allowing the young to take up life on their own. Like most algae, *Volvox* can reproduce in two ways. The first way, called asexual reproduction, happens when a single parent produces young. The second way, sexual reproduction, happens when male and female cells come together, making a fertilized egg cell.

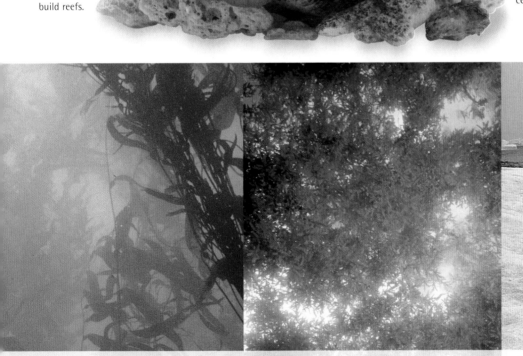

▲ GIANT KELP

Growing off the coastline of California, giant kelp creates towering underwater forests that are important habitats for wildlife. Giant kelp is the world's biggest seaweed, and in good conditions it can grow nearly 1 m (3¼ ft) a day. Like many kelps, it stays upright by growing gas-filled floats or bladders. In the Pacific Ocean, kelps are harvested for use as fertilizers. They also contain substances called alginates, which are used to thicken food.

▲ DRIFTING SEAWEEDS

Most seaweeds are attached to rocks or the sea bed, but sargassum weed drifts in open water. Large mats of it float in the Sargasso Sea, off the east coast of North America. In the early days of exploration, sailors were afraid that their ships would get tangled up in these mats. Sargassum weed creates a unique habitat for ocean wildlife. Many animals that live in it, such as the Sargassum fish, are camouflaged to match its fronds.

▲ SNOW ALGAE

This melting snow is stained pink by algae that live high up on mountains. Snow algae begin to grow in spring, as the days get longer and the snow starts to melt. They live just beneath the snow's surface, where they are protected from intense sunshine and from the worst of the night-time cold. Snow algae reproduce by making egg cells that are buried by fresh snow in winter. When the snow melts, their life cycle comes full circle as the egg cells start to grow.

FUNGI AND LICHENS

Fungi can sometimes look like plants, but they live in a very different way. Instead of making their own food, they feed on living things or their dead remains. Fungi spread by shedding spores, and they thrive in all kinds of habitats, from soil and wood to the surface of human skin. Some fungi are helpful partners for other living things, but many others cause diseases. Lichens are permanent partnerships between fungi and microscopic algae. They can survive tough conditions, and although they grow slowly, they sometimes live to a great age.

Domed cap keeps rainwater off the toadstool's gills

fungi

◄ TOADSTOOLS

A fungus's fruiting body is called a toadstool. Beneath the cap are vertical flaps, called gills, which produce spores. When the spores are ripe, the toadstool scatters them into the air. The rest of the fungus consists of a network of feeding threads, called hyphae, that is hidden away underground. Some toadstools are good to eat (we often call these mushrooms) but some, including the fly agarics shown here, are extremely poisonous.

Spore-producing gills are hidden beneath the cap

Stalk is a dense mass of tangled fungal threads

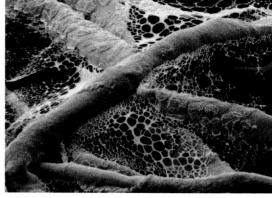

▲ HOW FUNGI FEED

Magnified hundreds of times, a fungus's hyphae (feeding threads) look like roots spreading through the soil. Unlike true roots, they grow through a fungus's food, digesting and absorbing any nutrients that they touch. A network of hyphae is called a mycelium. In suitable habitats, such as woodland soil, mycelia can form huge networks that grow from a single spore. Some of these networks cover over 600 ha (1,500 acres), making them the world's largest living things.

◄ SPREADING SPORES

When a puffball fruiting body (mushroom) is ripe, its head splits open to release clouds of dark brown spores. A single puffball can release over a thousand billion spores, each so small and light that it can drift far away on the breeze. Spores can stay alive for years, but they can grow only if they land on or very near their food. Most spores do not succeed, which is why fungi have to produce them in such huge numbers.

FRUITING BODIES

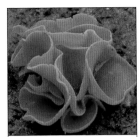

ORANGE-PEEL FUNGUS
This bright orange fungus lives on bare ground or wasteland. Also known as elf-cup fungus, it produces cup-shaped fruiting bodies that can be up to 10 cm (4 in) across. Orange-peel fungus makes its spores on the upper surface of the cup. When the spores are ripe, the fungus fires them towards the light.

SUMMER TRUFFLE
Truffles are one of the world's most expensive foods, famed for their delicious flavour. Their round or knobbly fruiting bodies develop underground, close to the roots of trees. Truffle spores are spread by animals, which dig down to feed on their flesh. Commercial truffle-hunters use trained dogs or pigs to find them.

JELLY ANTLER
This woodland fungus has fruiting bodies that look like bright yellow antlers. It grows on the rotting wood of dead conifers, usually on or near ground level. The jelly antler has several close relatives, which grow on different types of wood. Some of them look like upright sausages, without any branches or forks.

DEVIL'S FINGERS
This strangely shaped fungus has between four and eight bright red "fingers", which spread wide over the ground. The upper surfaces of the fingers are covered with slimy spores that smell like rotting meat. Their odour attracts flies, who crawl all over them. The spores stick to the flies' feet and are carried away.

BIRD'S-NEST FUNGUS
Instead of releasing spores into the air, the bird's-nest fungus grows them inside tiny, egglike objects. The eggs sit inside a cup that is shaped like a bird's nest, and they are catapulted out by falling raindrops. Bird's-nest fungus feeds on compost and other plant remains. It sometimes grows in flowerpots.

◄ YEAST
The waxy sheen on these ripe plums is produced by a layer of living yeast. Yeasts are single-celled fungi that feed on sugars. They multiply by growing small buds, which turn into new yeast cells. Yeasts give off carbon dioxide as they feed. They are useful for baking, because they can make dough rise, and for fermenting alcoholic drinks, such as beer and wine.

Bread mould spores form a fruiting body or cap

◄ MOULDS
This slice of stale bread has been invaded by moulds. A mould is a fungus that does not produce large toadstools. Some moulds are flat, but bread mould grows fruiting bodies that look like fine tufts of hair. Many moulds digest living plants or their dead remains, but some live on artificial materials, such as damp plaster, wallpaper paste, or even the coatings of camera lenses.

ATTACKING PLANTS ►
With its yellowing leaves and bare branches, this elm tree does not have long to live. It has Dutch elm disease, a fungal infection that is spread by bark beetles. Many other fungi attack plants. Mould spores cause potato blight, a devastating disease that destroys potato crops. It caused famine in Ireland in the mid-1800s and still affects potato crops today.

◄ PENICILLIN
This greenish mould, *Penicillium*, feeds on ripe fruit and plant remains. As it grows, it releases a chemical called penicillin, which keeps bacteria at bay. Penicillin is a valuable drug, because it kills bacteria that cause human diseases, without harming people themselves. Drugs that act in this way are called antibiotics. Penicillin was the first antibiotic to be discovered, in 1928.

ATTACKING ANIMALS ►
This moth has been killed by *Cordyceps* fungus, whose fruiting bodies look like a fur coat. Remarkably, fungi like this can even change their victims' behaviour. The victim may go and die high up on a plant, where the fungus will be able to scatter its spores. Fungi attack many other animals, including people. For example, ringworm is a fungus that infects human skin.

LICHENS ►
Compared to plants, lichens grow slowly, but they survive in some of the harshest habitats on Earth. Many grow on bare rocks, walls, or tree trunks, and some manage to survive within 1,200 km (745 miles) of the South Pole. Lichens can be flat, or upright and bushy, like tiny shrubs. The outer part of a lichen is made up by a fungus, which collects nutrients and water. The inner part contains microscopic algae, which make food by photosynthesis.

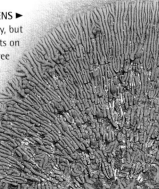

SEEDLESS PLANTS

The world's simplest land plants do not have flowers or seeds. Instead, they reproduce by releasing tiny cells called spores. Spores are far smaller and simpler than seeds, and they spread by water or on the wind. Seedless plants include liverworts, mosses, and horsetails, as well as all the world's ferns (see pages 30–31). Unlike seed plants, a seedless plant's life cycle alternates between two distinct plant forms: one that produces spores, and one that produces sex cells (sperm and eggs). Sometimes the two plant forms look similar, but often they are completely different, both in size and shape.

MOSSES ▶
This gnarled oak is covered with bright green moss. There are more than 9,000 kinds of mosses, and they are common in places that are shady, damp, and cool. Together with liverworts, mosses make up a group of plants called bryophytes. These plants do not have true roots and they collect water through their surface. Many moss plants are upright, with small scales that look like leaves. They release their spores from tiny capsules, which grow on slender stalks.

seedless
plants

◀ LIVERWORTS
Liverworts are the world's simplest true plants. Many of them look like small green ribbons, which branch in two as they grow. Like mosses, liverworts do not have true roots and can grow on surfaces without soil. Liverworts reproduce by making spores, but many also spread by growing egg-shaped beads, called gemmae, which sit in tiny cups. If a raindrop lands in the cup, the beads are splashed out and away from the parent plant.

SINGLE CUP CONTAINING
GEMMAE

PLANTS FROM THE PAST

These pointed scales come from the fossilized bark of a giant club moss, which lived more than 280 million years ago. At that time, seedless plants were much bigger than they are today. Horsetails grew to almost 20 m (65½ ft) high, and giant club mosses reached 35 m (115 ft) or more. Vast forests of these plants grew in swampy ground, leaving dead remains that eventually turned into coal.

MOSS SPORES

PEAT MOSSES ►

Unlike typical mosses, peat mosses grow in places that are waterlogged. They form green or pink mounds, sometimes over 1 m (3¼ ft) across, that appear solid but give way under the slightest weight. In the past, peat mosses were harvested for packing and bandages. Once dry, they soak up water better than a sponge.

PEAT BOGS ►

This mechanical cutter is slicing up peat – a crumbly substance formed in bogs from dead mosses and other plant remains. Over thousands of years, peat builds up into layers up to 10 m (33 ft) deep. Peatland is important for wildlife around the world but it is disappearing fast. When it is dug up and dried out, peat can be burned as a fuel.

CLUB MOSSES ►

Most club mosses live on forest floors, but this one, the resurrection plant, grows in deserts, and comes to life after it rains. Despite their name, club mosses are not close relatives of true mosses, and they are built differently. They have true roots and stems, so they are able to collect water from the soil and also grow taller.

HORSETAILS ►

Named for their upright stems and stiff, hairlike leaves, horsetails can form dense clumps on moist, fertile ground. The largest kind, from South America, grows 10 m (33 ft) high. There are only about 30 kinds of horsetail around today, and some have changed very little in over 300 million years.

◄ SPORES

Clustered on the surface of a moss, these spores will soon blow away in the wind. Each spore consists of a single cell, surrounded by a tough outer coat. Spores are so small that they can float far away on the slightest breeze. They can survive for years in dry conditions, but as soon as they are moist, they start to grow. Seedless plants are not the only things that produce spores: bacteria, fungi, and algae make them as well.

Tough casing protects
the spore cell inside

FERNS

There are more than 10,000 kinds of ferns, and they make up the biggest group of seedless plants. Some are only ankle-high, but the tallest have trunks like trees. Unlike simpler plants, such as mosses and liverworts, ferns have true roots and stems. Their leaves, or fronds, are often divided into separate leaflets, which gives them their ferny shape. Most ferns live in damp habitats, but some float on freshwater. Like other seedless plants, they reproduce by releasing spores, and their life cycles involve two separate forms of plant.

◄ HOW FERN FRONDS GROW
Fern fronds sprout from a fibrous stem or trunk. When the fronds are young, they are coiled up tightly in a shape called a fiddlehead. As each frond grows, the fiddlehead uncoils until the frond is spread out straight. In warm parts of the world, ferns grow new fronds all the time, and some of their fronds last for several years. In places with cold winters, most ferns die down in autumn, and then sprout new fronds in the spring.

Fiddlehead
(young frond)
is tightly coiled

Central stem
supports the frond

ferns

▲ TREE FERNS
These are the world's tallest ferns, and the largest seedless plants. They have a single, branchless trunk and elegant fronds that can be over 2.5 m (8¼ ft) long. Most tree ferns grow in shady forests. They are found throughout the tropics, and also in cooler regions in the southern half of the world, such as Tasmania and New Zealand. Old specimens can be 25 m (82 ft) high.

▲ FILMY FERNS
These small ferns get their name from their delicate fronds, which are only one or two cells thick in the parts between their veins. Fronds this thin dry out easily, so filmy ferns live in very damp places such as rain-soaked forests, shaded river banks, and around waterfalls. Filmy ferns often grow by creeping over the ground.

THE LIFE CYCLE OF A FERN

DEVELOPING
SPOROPHYTE

MATURE
SPOROPHYTE

SINGLE-CELL
SPOROPHYTE

FERTILIZATION

DEVELOPING
SPORANGIA

POUCH CONTAINING
FEMALE SEX CELL

MALE
SEX
CELL

MATURE
GAMETOPHYTE

SPORES
RELEASED

GERMINATING
SPORE

POUCH OF
MALE SEX CELLS

DEVELOPING
GAMETOPHYTE

A fern's life cycle alternates between two different forms of plant. One of these forms, called a sporophyte, is easy to spot because it has leafy fronds. Once it is mature, the sporophyte produces the fern's spores. These develop in tiny capsules called sporangia, which are arranged in clusters on the back of the fern's fronds. When the spores are ripe, the sporangia split open.

If a spore lands in a suitable spot, it germinates and the second plant form starts to grow. This is called a gametophyte, because it produces the fern's gametes, or sex cells. The gametophyte is usually thin and flat, and often no bigger than a stamp. Male and female sex cells develop in separate pouches on the gametophyte's underside. Male cells swim towards the female ones. Once fertilization has taken place, a new sporophyte is formed and it starts to push up its own leafy fronds.

FERN FRONDS

HART'S-TONGUE FERN
This fern has tongue-shaped fronds with flat or frilly edges. They can be up to 50 cm (19½ in) long, and they have velvety lines on their undersides, containing the microscopic capsules that make their spores. A close relative of this species, the bird's-nest fern, has giant fronds up to 1.5 m (5 ft) long. It comes from the tropics, but it is often grown as a house plant.

COMMON POLYPODY
Like most ferns, common polypody has fronds that are divided into lots of smaller leaflets, which gives them a feathery shape. Its fronds can be 40 cm (15¾ in) long. They have raised dots on their undersides containing capsules that make the spores. Common polypody sometimes grows on the ground, but the best places to see it are on trees, rocks, and the tops of old stone walls.

ROYAL FERN
With its majestic fronds, the royal fern is often cultivated as a garden plant. Each frond is doubly divided, meaning that each leaflet is split into leaflets itself. It has special spore-producing fronds that grow up in the middle of the plant. Unlike the rest of its fronds, these are narrow and rusty brown. Royal fern is native to boggy places and grows in many different parts of the world.

▲ BRACKEN
Some ferns are rare and endangered, but bracken is a successful weed. It spreads by underground stems and forms large clumps in woodlands and fields. Bracken is poisonous to farm animals, and it is hard to get rid of because its buried stems soon regrow. Unusually for a fern, bracken is found all over the world.

▲ EPIPHYTIC FERNS
Ferns that perch on other plants are called epiphytes. There are thousands of kinds, mostly in the tropics. Measuring over 1 m (3¼ ft) across, this stag's-horn fern has narrow fronds that produce spores, and large fronds that hold it in place and catch falling leaves. As they rot, the leaves supply the fern with nutrients.

▲ WATER FERNS
Mosquito fern grows on the surface of pools and ponds – the habitat where mosquitoes breed. Its upper surface is water-repellent so it is hard to sink. In spring and summer, it is bluish-green. In autumn and winter, it turns red. There are many kinds of water fern. Most spread on the feet of water birds.

SEED PLANTS

Most plants spread by making seeds. Unlike a spore, a seed contains a complete embryo plant, together with a supply of food. The food keeps the embryo alive and gives it a head start when it begins to grow. There are two groups of seed plants. Conifers and their relatives make their seeds on special scales, which are packed together to form cones. Flowering plants produce seeds inside closed chambers called ovaries, which form part of their flowers. Whether they develop in cones or flowers, all seeds need protection and a way to spread.

◄ SEEDS FROM CONES
A pine cone is like a seed-making factory, built out of a spiral of woody scales. Each one makes a pair of seeds on its underside. When the seeds are ripe, the scales open out so their seeds can flutter away. Plants that grow cones have existed for over 300 million years – much longer than plants that make seeds by growing flowers.

Scale gradually opens out in warm weather

Seed is attached to a long, transparent wing

seed plants

▼ SPREADING BY SEEDS
All over the world, seed plants dominate the scenery. This sunbaked hillside in southern Europe contains dozens of different seed plants. In the foreground are flowering shrubs, including rockroses, spurges, and brooms. Behind them are wind-sculpted tree heathers and pines. To make seeds, all these plants have to exchange pollen with plants of their own kind.

Exposed branches grow away from the prevailing wind

Tree spurge often sheds its leaves in summer

FROM BUD TO SEED

BUD
Flowers have many parts and can take weeks to form. While it develops, the flower is protected inside a bud. In most plants, each bud is protected by green flaps called sepals. This poppy bud has two sepals, which fit together like a case. When the flower is ready to open, the sepals fold apart and then fall to the ground.

FLOWER
Insects visit a poppy flower to collect its pollen and also bring pollen from other poppies. Pollen grains contain male cells, which fertilize the plant's female cells, or ova. The ova are housed in the ovary, a chamber in the middle of the flower. Once the flower has been pollinated, its petals drop and the seeds start to grow.

MATURE SEED HEAD
Three weeks later, the ovary has swelled up to form a round seed head. The seed head is hard and dry, with the seeds loose inside. As the seed head ripens, its lid arches upwards, and a ring of holes opens up beneath its rim. If the wind shakes the seed head, the seeds sprinkle through the holes like pepper from a pepper pot.

SEEDS
A single poppy plant can produce over 5,000 seeds. Each one has a hard case that protects the embryo plant inside. The embryo is alive, but it does not start to grow until the conditions outside are exactly right. It stays dormant, sometimes for many years, but as soon as the soil is moist and warm, the seed will germinate.

MICROSCOPIC SEEDS ►
The world's smallest seeds belong to orchids – 5,000 of them together weigh only as much as a single poppy seed. Orchid seeds are so small that they cannot be seen without a microscope. They have very little room for food reserves. Instead, they depend on soil-dwelling fungi to help them germinate and grow. Most seedlings produce leaves as quickly as they can, but young orchids can take several years to sprout above ground.

Orchid seed magnified 140 times

HIDDEN VARIATIONS ►
From the outside, a plant's seeds may look identical. Inside, each embryo has its own unique set of genes. As a result, adult plants are different too. These bluebells show one kind of variation: some have pink flowers instead of the normal blue. Genetic variation allows plants to adapt and evolve. Plants (and all living things) adapt to their changing surroundings by evolving.

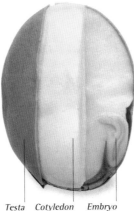

◄ INSIDE A SEED
This broad bean has been sliced open to show the different parts inside a seed. The entire seed is surrounded by a tough outer coat called a testa. Further inside are two waxy coloured seed leaves called cotyledons. These contain the seed's store of food. The embryo is between the cotyledons. It has a tiny shoot and also the beginnings of a root. The root is the first part to emerge when the seed germinates.

Testa (seed coat) *Cotyledon (seed leaf) contains food store* *Embryo*

SEEDS AS FOOD ►
For this grey squirrel – and many other animals – seeds are an important source of food. They are rich in nutrients and easy to store away as a reserve for hungry times. Squirrels often bury nuts in the autumn and dig them up in winter, when food is hard to find. This can help trees, because squirrels forget about some of the nuts. When spring comes, they are in just the right place to start growing.

Grey squirrel eats seeds such as hazelnuts

◄ GIANT SEEDS
The world's largest seeds belong to the double coconut palm or coco de mer. This palm tree grows in the Seychelles, a group of islands in the Indian Ocean. Each of its seeds is surrounded by a gigantic cleft (divided) husk. The seed and husk together weigh up to 20 kg (44 lb) – as much as a six-year-old child. These gigantic seeds take seven years to mature on the tree, before they finally fall off and hit the ground.

CONIFEROUS PLANTS

There are less than 800 different kinds of gymnosperm (coniferous plant), compared to more than 250,000 kinds of flowering plant. Gymnosperms grow all across the world and are good at surviving in harsh habitats such as mountains, deserts, and the cold regions near the poles. Unlike flowering plants, coniferous plants grow their seeds in cones, and they spread their seeds and pollen by scattering them into the wind. Most coniferous plants are trees or shrubs, and they include the world's tallest and heaviest living things.

e ▶▶ coniferous plants

Male cones ready to release pollen

Unfertilized female cone

Mature female cone has hard, brown scales

Young female cone with soft, green scales was fertilized a year ago

◄ CONIFERS
This Scots pine is a typical conifer, with a slender trunk and tough evergreen leaves. Conifers make up three-quarters of all coniferous plants or gymnosperms. They include many trees that are grown for timber, such as pines, spruces, and firs, as well as cedars, redwoods, and yews. Compared to some conifers, the Scots pine is widespread. It grows across a large part of Europe and northern Asia.

CONES ►
Conifers grow two different types of cones. Their male cones are small and soft. When they are ripe, they shed clouds of pollen into the air, then wither away. Female cones are soft when they are young, but they often become hard and woody as they grow. Once they have been pollinated, they produce seeds. Pine cones usually fall to the ground in one piece, but the upright cones of firs and cedars break up as their seeds are released.

CONIFER LEAVES

NEEDLES
Pines have slender, pointed leaves known as needles that grow in clusters of up to eight. They usually stay on the tree for up to four years, but in some species – such as the bristlecone pine – they can last 30 years or more. Their waxy surface helps to stop them drying out and protects them from cold winds.

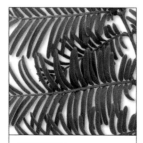

FLAT LEAVES
Like many conifers, the dawn redwood has narrow, flattened leaves. Flat leaves often have a shiny top surface and pale underside. Most conifers are evergreen, but the dawn redwood is deciduous. It loses its leaves in autumn and grows a new set in spring. Larches, which have needle-shaped leaves, are also deciduous.

SCALES
A wide range of conifers, from cypresses to redwoods, have small, scale-shaped leaves. These leaves come from a hiba, a conifer that grows in the mountain forests of Japan. Scaly leaves can collect lots of light. Some conifers, such as junipers, have needles when they are young, but scaly leaves when they are mature.

▲ FLESHY FRUIT
Yews and their relatives are different from other conifers. Instead of having hard cones, their seeds sit in a colourful, fleshy cup called an aril, which looks like a berry. Yew berries are poisonous to humans and farm animals, but birds eat them without coming to any harm. By doing this, they help to spread yew seeds in their droppings. Yew trees are either male or female, and only the female ones have berry-like arils.

▲ BOREAL FOREST
Stretching across North America, Europe, and northern Asia, the boreal (northern) forest is the largest forest in the world. Its extra-tough conifers can withstand bitter winters lasting up to eight months each year. The trees have a pointed shape, which helps snow to slide off instead of building up on their branches. The forest interior is dark and silent, with boggy ground that makes it difficult to explore.

▲ CALIFORNIAN GIANTS
Soaring up into the sky, these coast redwoods from California are the world's tallest trees. The record-holder is currently 112 m (367 ft) high and at least 1,000 years old. Coast redwoods grow so tall because they never run short of moisture. There is plenty of rain and fog on the coast. The fog turns into water droplets on the trees' leaves, dripping onto the ground far below.

CYCADS ▲
Often confused with palm trees, cycads are coniferous plants that have existed for over 300 million years. They have short trunks, topped by a crown of stiff, feather-shaped leaves. They grow cones at the tops of their trunks, with male and female ones on separate plants. Most cycads live in warm parts of the world, from Florida to Australia. Cycads grow very slowly. Many species have become endangered because they are dug up and sold as garden plants.

WELWITSCHIA ▼
The welwitschia, from Africa's Namib Desert, is one of the strangest plants in the world. It can live for over 1,000 years, and it has just two long, curling leaves, which sprout from a waist-high trunk. The leaves are as hard as wood, and they crack and split as they grow. After several centuries, the plant looks more like a heap of rubbish than a living thing. Welwitschias grow their cones on small branches, which sprout from the base of their leaves.

Finger-sized cones grow in small clusters

Deep, water-storing taproot is hidden below ground

Leaf grows from its base at the centre of the plant

Oldest leaf parts are split and frayed

FLOWERING PLANTS

Wherever you are on Earth, flowering plants are never far away. There are more than 250,000 species, found in all kinds of habitats. Flowering plants are known as angiosperms, which means "seed cases". Their seeds grow inside ovaries (closed chambers at the centre of their flowers). Angiosperms split into two groups – monocotyledons, which have one seed leaf, and dicotyledons, which have two.

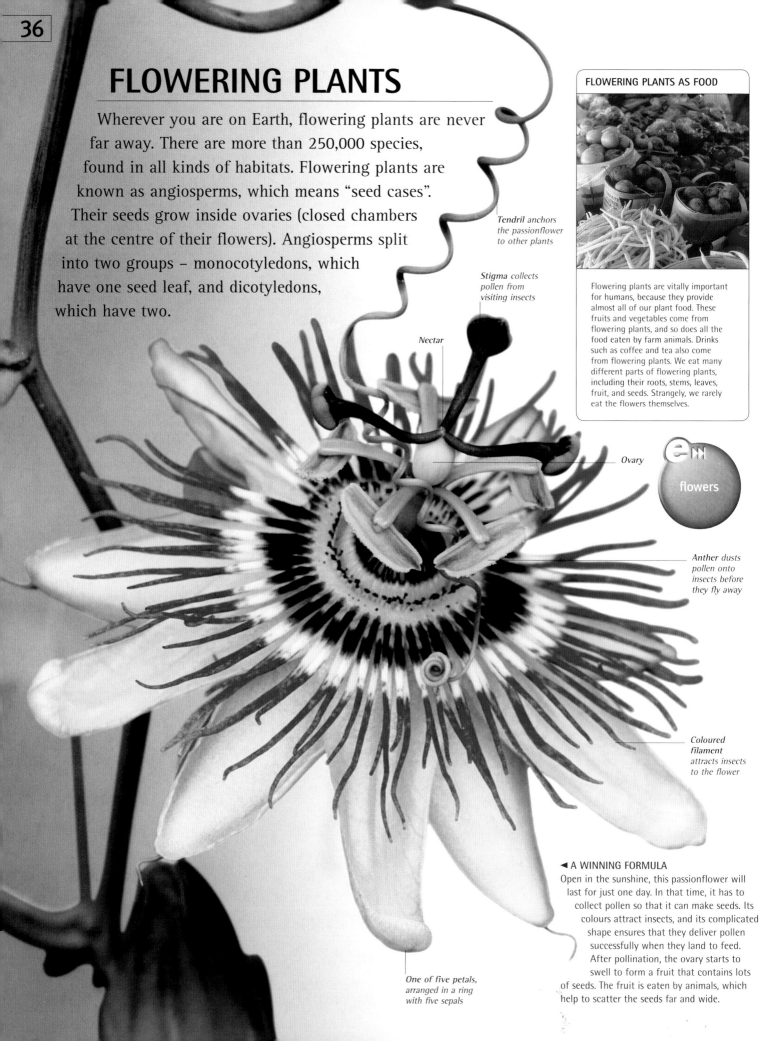

Tendril anchors the passionflower to other plants

Stigma collects pollen from visiting insects

Nectar

Ovary

flowers

Anther dusts pollen onto insects before they fly away

Coloured filament attracts insects to the flower

One of five petals, arranged in a ring with five sepals

FLOWERING PLANTS AS FOOD

Flowering plants are vitally important for humans, because they provide almost all of our plant food. These fruits and vegetables come from flowering plants, and so does all the food eaten by farm animals. Drinks such as coffee and tea also come from flowering plants. We eat many different parts of flowering plants, including their roots, stems, leaves, fruit, and seeds. Strangely, we rarely eat the flowers themselves.

◄ A WINNING FORMULA
Open in the sunshine, this passionflower will last for just one day. In that time, it has to collect pollen so that it can make seeds. Its colours attract insects, and its complicated shape ensures that they deliver pollen successfully when they land to feed. After pollination, the ovary starts to swell to form a fruit that contains lots of seeds. The fruit is eaten by animals, which help to scatter the seeds far and wide.

Fleshy petal

Stigmas form central column

Anthers at base of flower

▲ THE FIRST FLOWERING PLANTS
This magnolia bloom is similar to the world's first flowers, which appeared between 130 and 140 million years ago. Early flowers had a ring of petals, and male and female parts in the middle. Many flowers have since evolved much more complicated shapes. Some have feathery anthers that scatter pollen in the air. Others, such as the passionflower, work like landing platforms for their animal visitors.

FLOWERING PLANT GROUPS

MONOCOTYLEDONS
These crocuses are monocotyledons (or monocots). They have a single cotyledon (seed leaf) prepacked inside their seeds. Monocots' adult leaves are often long and narrow, with parallel veins. Their flower parts are usually in multiples of three. Monocots include grasses, lilies, orchids, and palms. Many grow from bulbs, and apart from palms, very few of them are trees.

DICOTYLEDONS
These rockroses are dicotyledons (or dicots), and so are over three-quarters of the world's flowering plants. They have two seed leaves. Dicots' adult leaves have a network of veins. Their flower parts are often in multiples of four or five. Dicots include many kinds of shrub, and also most of the world's broad-leaved trees. Unlike monocots, many have deep taproots.

▲ GIANT FLOWERING PLANTS
With their dead-straight trunks, mountain ashes are the world's tallest flowering plants. These majestic trees are a kind of eucalyptus that grows in cool, damp parts of Australia. The tallest living mountain ash is 93 m (305 ft) high, but larger ones existed in the past. In the 1800s, foresters found fallen mountain ashes over 140 m (459 ft) long. When they were alive, they were probably the tallest plants the world has ever seen.

▲ MINIATURE FLOWERING PLANTS
This pond is covered with duckweeds – the smallest flowering plants in the world. Duckweeds drift on the surface of the water like little green beads. Instead of leaves, each plant has a tiny frond that works like a float. The smallest species of duckweed, *Wolffia*, is less than 1 mm ($^{1}/_{30}$ in) long. It has no roots, and its flowers are too tiny to see with the naked eye.

Duckweed floats on the surface of the water

◄ FLOWERS IN THE SEA
Lots of flowering plants grow in freshwater, but very few can survive in the sea. One of the exceptions is sea grass, which grows not far from the shoreline. This pipefish is swimming in a sea-grass meadow. Sea grass has tiny flowers, and it is pollinated underwater. It is an important food for many sea animals, including fish and turtles. Pipefish and sea horses use sea-grass meadows as a place to feed and to hide.

FLOWERS

Flowers are the most eye-catching parts of plants. They contain a plant's reproductive organs and their job is to exchange pollen, so that they can make seeds. Some flowers use the wind to spread their pollen, but flowers that are big, bright, or strongly scented use animals. Many plants grow their flowers singly, but some produce them in groups called flower heads. A flower head can have less than a dozen individual flowers, but the biggest contain tens of thousands, attracting pollinating animals from far and wide.

flowers

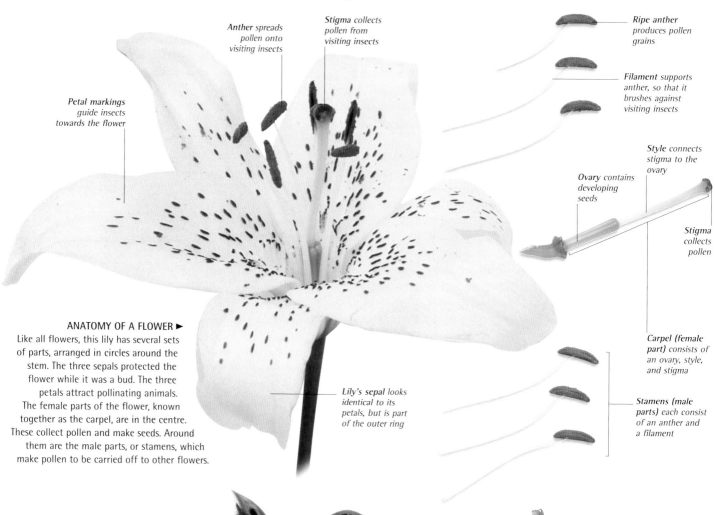

Anther spreads pollen onto visiting insects

Stigma collects pollen from visiting insects

Petal markings guide insects towards the flower

Ripe anther produces pollen grains

Filament supports anther, so that it brushes against visiting insects

Style connects stigma to the ovary

Ovary contains developing seeds

Stigma collects pollen

ANATOMY OF A FLOWER ▶
Like all flowers, this lily has several sets of parts, arranged in circles around the stem. The three sepals protected the flower while it was a bud. The three petals attract pollinating animals. The female parts of the flower, known together as the carpel, are in the centre. These collect pollen and make seeds. Around them are the male parts, or stamens, which make pollen to be carried off to other flowers.

Lily's sepal looks identical to its petals, but is part of the outer ring

Carpel (female part) consists of an ovary, style, and stigma

Stamens (male parts) each consist of an anther and a filament

SEPARATE SEXES ▶
Some flowering plants produce male and female flowers on separate plants. The male plants produce pollen, while females produce fruit and seeds – such as these holly berries. Plants like this are called dioecious, a word that means "two houses". Dioecious plants include willows, kiwi fruit, asparagus, and palms. To produce seeds, the female plants need pollen, so there have to be male plants growing nearby.

MALE FLOWER

FEMALE FLOWER

◀ SEXES TOGETHER
Unlike animals, most plants are male and female at the same time. Plants like this are called monoecious, a word that means "one house". On this courgette plant, separate male and female flowers grow on the same plant. However, most monoecious plants have flowers with both male and female parts. When these flowers open, the male parts often ripen first. This helps to stop the flowers from pollinating themselves.

FLOWER HEADS

SPIKE

The Australian bottlebrush plant has flower heads called spikes. In a spike, the flowers grow directly from a long stalk, instead of having their own stems. Spikes often point straight upwards but one common type, called a catkin, does the opposite and hangs down. In a bottlebrush spike, the individual flowers have tiny petals, but long, colourful stamens. These attract pollinating birds, which feed on the nectar in the flowers.

RACEME

The graceful flowers of bluebells and hyacinths make up a type of flower head called a raceme. A raceme is like a spike, but each flower grows on its own short stem. In a raceme, the lowest flowers often open first, while the ones higher up are still in bud. This arrangement is useful for insects and other pollinating animals, because the flower head can keep providing them with food for several weeks.

PANICLE

Like many other grasses, rice grows its flowers in panicles. A panicle is like a raceme, but each side branch has branches of its own, each ending in a flower. The result is a large cluster of flowers growing side by side. Some panicles can be gigantic. The talipot palm from southeast Asia grows panicles up to 5 m (30 ft) high, containing hundreds of thousands of flowers. After producing its seeds, the palm dies.

UMBEL

Umbels are easy flower heads to recognize because they are umbrella-shaped, with stalks like spokes. These umbels belong to a wild carrot plant. Most of its relatives, such as hogweed, fennel, and celery, have umbels as well. In an umbel, the flowers are often shallow, and they open at the same time. This creates a large landing platform for pollinating insects, such as small beetles, midges, and hover flies.

SPADIX

This skunk cabbage has tiny flowers, which grow in a fleshy column called a spadix. Around the spadix is a hood, known as a spathe. The spadix gives off a powerful smell, and the spathe helps to steer small insects towards the flowers, so that they are pollinated. All the skunk cabbage's relatives – which include the Swiss cheese plant, arum lily, and calla lily – have this unusual kind of flower head.

OPENING TIMES

Flowers are tougher than they look, but they can still be damaged by rain or cold. Like many flowers, this dandelion opens up during the day, but closes in the evening for extra protection against the night-time cold. Some flowers close up when it starts to rain, or even when the sky turns cloudy.

Flowers that are pollinated by nocturnal animals, such as moths or bats, work the other way around. They often open at dusk, stay open all night, and close shortly after dawn. These flowers are often highly scented, but they produce their scent only at night, when their animal visitors are on the wing.

COMPOSITE FLOWERS ►

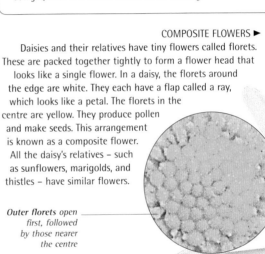

Daisies and their relatives have tiny flowers called florets. These are packed together tightly to form a flower head that looks like a single flower. In a daisy, the florets around the edge are white. They each have a flap called a ray, which looks like a petal. The florets in the centre are yellow. They produce pollen and make seeds. This arrangement is known as a composite flower. All the daisy's relatives – such as sunflowers, marigolds, and thistles – have similar flowers.

Outer florets open first, followed by those nearer the centre

Sepal

Sepal moves apart from other sepals as flower opens

Petal expands and folds back

Nasturtium flower has five petals

Ovary is in the centre of the flower

◄ A FLOWER OPENS

Most flower buds are protected by green flaps called sepals. When the flower opens, the sepals may stay in place or fall to the ground. The petals quickly expand, folding back as they grow. The last parts to mature are the stamens and carpels. In many flowers, these ripen at different times, to make it more likely that the flower will be pollinated by another flower's pollen.

ANIMAL POLLINATION

Before a flower can make seeds, its female cells have to be fertilized by male pollen grains. Flowers sometimes pollinate themselves, but the healthiest seeds are produced if the pollen is from another plant. Some flowers use the wind to spread their pollen, but many use insects or other animals. They attract them with bright colours, strong smells, and sweet, liquid nectar. When an animal arrives to feed, it dusts pollen onto the female parts of the flower. The male parts of the flower brush it with pollen, which it carries to another flower.

Pollen grains stick to the bee's foot

Small claw at tip of foot

BUMBLEBEE'S FOOT

◄ POLLINATION
In many parts of the world, bumblebees are the first pollinating insects to start work in the spring. As they fly from flower to flower, microscopic pollen grains stick to their feet and fur-like scales. When they land on a flower, bees deliver some of this pollen, allowing the flower to make seeds. In return, the flower gives the bee a meal of nectar. Many bees also collect surplus pollen to feed to their grubs.

POLLEN GERMINATION ON A POPPY STIGMA

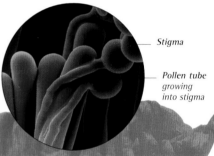

Stigma

Pollen tube growing into stigma

Stigma
Pollen tube
Ovules

POPPY FLOWER

POLLEN GRAINS

ELM POLLEN
Pollen grains are as distinctive as fingerprints, because each kind of plant produces a different type. This grain is from an elm tree – a plant that is pollinated by the wind. Elm pollen is light and dusty, so that it blows far and wide through the air. Each grain is covered by a tough outer coat, with a single hole or pore.

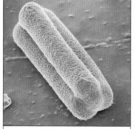

CROSSANDRA POLLEN
This pollen grain, with three long lobes, is from a colourful shrub called crossandra that grows in tropical Africa. Crossandra flowers are pollinated by insects. Each pollen grain is very sticky so that it will fix to visiting insects. Like all pollen grains, it contains two male cells – enough to form a single seed.

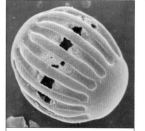

MILKWORT POLLEN
A grain of milkwort pollen is rounded, with a set of ridges and furrows. Like crossandra pollen, the grain sticks to insects' feet or hairs. Despite their small size, pollen grains are extremely tough. If they are buried, they keep their shape for thousands of years, allowing scientists to investigate plants of the past.

◄ FERTILIZATION
For fertilization to happen, a pollen grain has to land on the stigma (female part) of the right kind of flower. Within hours, the pollen grain germinates and produces a slender pollen tube. The tube grows down into the flower's ovary, where it inserts two male cells into a female ovule (egg cell). One of the male cells fertilizes the ovule to form an embryo. The other helps to build the endosperm – a tissue that the embryo uses as food. This is called double fertilization, and it is found only in flowering plants.

FLOWER IN
ORDINARY
DAYLIGHT

FLOWER IN
ULTRAVIOLET
LIGHT

*Markings
only visible
to insects*

▲ NECTAR GUIDES

These two photographs show the same flower lit in two different ways. At the top, the flower is in normal daylight. To human eyes, it looks plain yellow with a dark centre. On the right, the flower is lit by ultraviolet light. This time, hidden markings are revealed. We cannot see ultraviolet light, but insects can. They follow these markings, known as nectar guides, to find the nectar at the centre of the flower.

◄ CARRION FLOWERS

In the deserts of southern Africa, carrion flowers lure flies by looking and smelling like rotting flesh. Their five petals are brown and fleshy, and they have a coat of soft bristles that feel just like fur. The flowers are over 20 cm (8 in) across and they open on the ground, which is exactly where flies search for dead remains. When a fly lands, the flower clips a package of pollen onto its legs. The fly then takes off, delivering the pollen to the next carrion flower that it visits.

▲ OPEN INVITATION

Umbels (umbrella-shaped flowers) are popular with all kinds of insects, from flies and beetles to bees and wasps. Flowers such as this hogweed receive thousands of visitors a day, which help them to spread their pollen. However, their pollen may be carried to the wrong kind of plant because their insect visitors are not fussy about where they feed. To avoid this problem, many plants have evolved special partnerships with pollinating animals.

*Yucca moth is
about to pollinate
the flower*

*Pollen grains at
the end of the
flower's anther*

▲ PRIVATE PARTNERSHIPS

Yucca flowers are pollinated by a single kind of insect – the pale-coloured yucca moth. The moth lays its eggs in yucca flowers, pollinating them as it flutters from plant to plant. Its caterpillars grow up inside the flowers. They eat some of the yucca seeds but leave the rest unharmed. After millions of years of living together, yuccas and their moths have become such close partners that they cannot survive without each other.

pollination

◄ BIRD POLLINATION

Hovering close to a bromeliad flower, this hummingbird is drinking a meal of sugary nectar. As it feeds, its beak becomes dusted with pollen, which it carries from flower to flower. Hummingbirds are found only in the Americas, but other pollinating birds live in different parts of the world. They include sunbirds in Africa, and honeyeaters and parrots in southeast Asia and Australia. Bird-pollinated flowers are often red, because this is a colour that birds see well.

*Wing of hovering
hummingbird
beats up to
80 times
a second*

*Straw-like beak
allows bird to suck
up nectar*

*Tube-shaped
flower fits
bird's beak*

▲ BAT POLLINATION

In warm parts of the world, bats are important pollinators of plants – particularly trees. This bat, a grey-headed flying fox, has landed on a eucalyptus tree in eastern Australia and is lapping up nectar and pollen with its long tongue. Bat-pollinated flowers are usually pale, to show up well in the dark, and often have a strong, musky scent. Bat-pollinated flowers have to be tough, because bats clamber about in them as they feed.

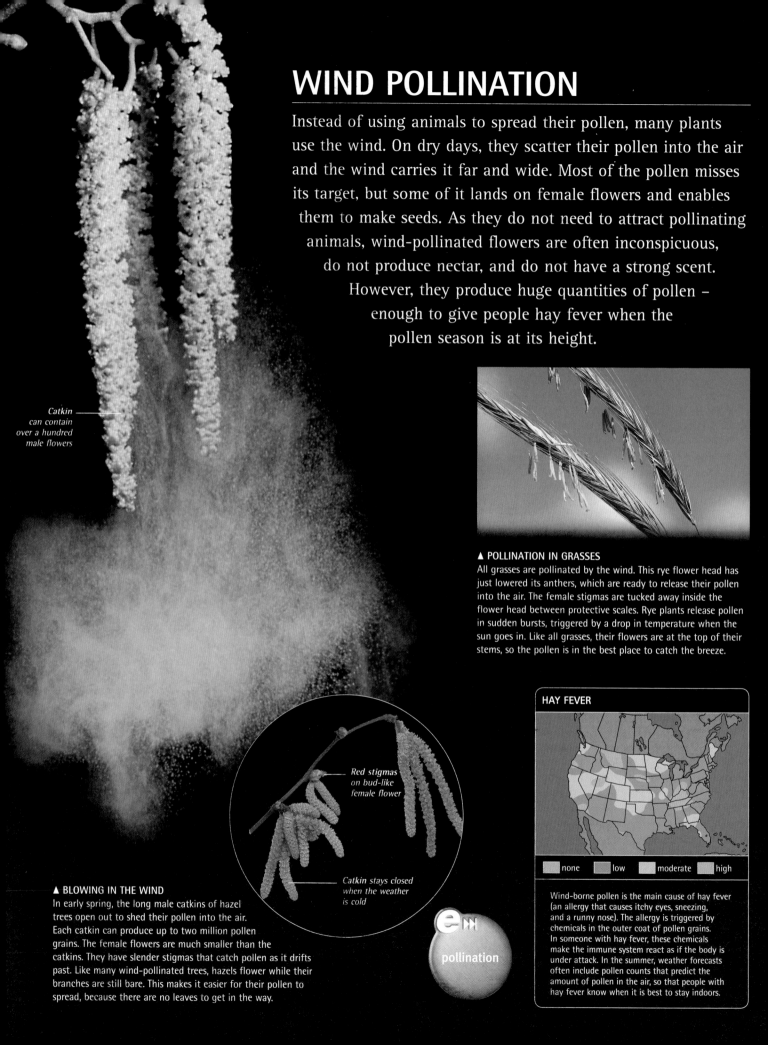

WIND POLLINATION

Instead of using animals to spread their pollen, many plants use the wind. On dry days, they scatter their pollen into the air and the wind carries it far and wide. Most of the pollen misses its target, but some of it lands on female flowers and enables them to make seeds. As they do not need to attract pollinating animals, wind-pollinated flowers are often inconspicuous, do not produce nectar, and do not have a strong scent. However, they produce huge quantities of pollen – enough to give people hay fever when the pollen season is at its height.

Catkin can contain over a hundred male flowers

▲ POLLINATION IN GRASSES

All grasses are pollinated by the wind. This rye flower head has just lowered its anthers, which are ready to release their pollen into the air. The female stigmas are tucked away inside the flower head between protective scales. Rye plants release pollen in sudden bursts, triggered by a drop in temperature when the sun goes in. Like all grasses, their flowers are at the top of their stems, so the pollen is in the best place to catch the breeze.

Red stigmas on bud-like female flower

Catkin stays closed when the weather is cold

HAY FEVER

■ none ■ low ■ moderate ■ high

▲ BLOWING IN THE WIND

In early spring, the long male catkins of hazel trees open out to shed their pollen into the air. Each catkin can produce up to two million pollen grains. The female flowers are much smaller than the catkins. They have slender stigmas that catch pollen as it drifts past. Like many wind-pollinated trees, hazels flower while their branches are still bare. This makes it easier for their pollen to spread, because there are no leaves to get in the way.

e▶▶
pollination

Wind-borne pollen is the main cause of hay fever (an allergy that causes itchy eyes, sneezing, and a runny nose). The allergy is triggered by chemicals in the outer coat of pollen grains. In someone with hay fever, these chemicals make the immune system react as if the body is under attack. In the summer, weather forecasts often include pollen counts that predict the amount of pollen in the air, so that people with hay fever know when it is best to stay indoors.

WIND-POLLINATED PLANTS

OAK

There are more than 600 kinds of oak tree and all of them are pollinated by the wind. Each oak tree has separate male and female flowers. The male flowers are in long hanging catkins, while the female ones are in smaller clusters near the tips of the branches. After flowering, the male catkins fall off, while the female flowers produce a crop of fruits called acorns.

HICKORY

Hickory female flowers are small and difficult to spot, but their male catkins are more eye-catching, despite being green. Hickories flower in spring, and their female flowers produce egg-shaped fruit containing hard-shelled nuts. There are about 20 species of hickory. One of them, the pecan, is grown in orchards in the southeastern USA.

POPLAR

The poplar family includes cottonwoods and aspens. Most poplars flower before they come into leaf. Unlike oaks or hickories, their male and female flowers grow on separate trees. After they have been pollinated, the female catkins often look like furry caterpillars. Each one contains dozens of tiny seeds, which float away on the wind on feathery hairs.

REED MACE

This common waterside plant is often confused with the bulrush, which also grows along the edges of ponds. The fat, brown part contains the female flowers. The male flowers are above them in a slender spike. When ripe, the male flowers look like straw-coloured cotton wool. In the autumn, the flower head breaks up, releasing seeds to be scattered by the wind.

RAGWEED

In North America, this wayside weed is notorious for causing hay fever. Since it thrives on disturbed ground, it is as common in cities as the open countryside. Its tassel-like male flowers are dull, green, and small, but in dry summer weather they release huge amounts of pollen into the air. After pollination the tiny, whiteish-green female flowers develop into prickly burs.

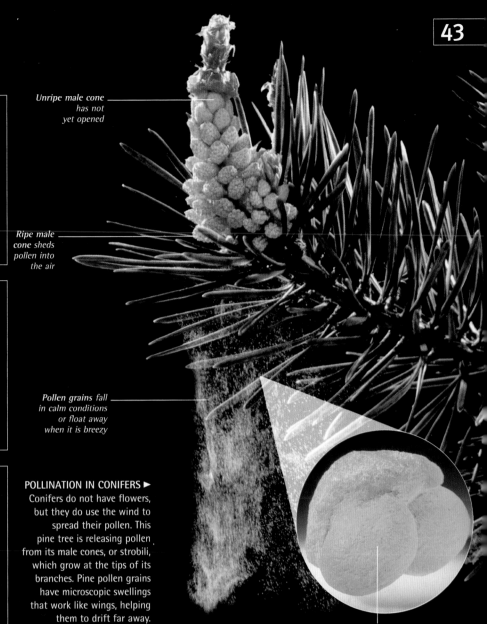

Unripe male cone has not yet opened

Ripe male cone sheds pollen into the air

Pollen grains fall in calm conditions or float away when it is breezy

Single pollen grain has rounded wings

POLLINATION IN CONIFERS ▶
Conifers do not have flowers, but they do use the wind to spread their pollen. This pine tree is releasing pollen from its male cones, or strobili, which grow at the tips of its branches. Pine pollen grains have microscopic swellings that work like wings, helping them to drift far away.

WATER POLLINATION

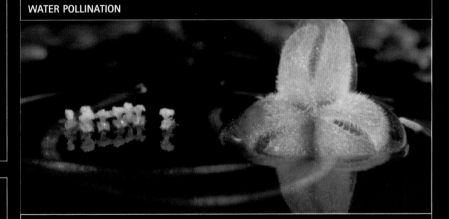

Most water plants flower above the surface and use animals or the wind to spread their pollen. Ribbonweed is different. Male ribbonweed plants flower underwater and release pollen in boat-like structures that bob up to the surface. Each of these structures has three petals that work like floats. The pollen boats drift across the water, moved by the slightest breeze.

Each female ribbonweed flower sits on the surface, waiting for the pollen boats to come its way. The surface tension of the water creates a dimple around the female flower which draws in any nearby pollen boats. Here, a row of pollen boats are about to be guided towards the centre of the flower.

Water-pollinated plants are also found in the sea. Sea grasses often have pollen grains with a wormlike shape. The pollen drifts through the water, until it becomes entangled in the female flowers.

HOW SEEDS SPREAD

Once a flower has been pollinated, it can form seeds. In flowering plants, seeds develop inside the flower's ovaries, and the result is known as a fruit. Fruits have many different sizes and shapes. They may be soft and juicy or hard and dry. The smallest fruits are no bigger than a pinhead, but the heaviest kinds – cultivated pumpkins – can weigh more than 600 kg (1,325 lb). Fruits protect seeds while they develop. Once the seeds are ripe, a fruit often helps its seeds to spread far away from the parent plant.

FLESHY FRUITS ▶
Using its huge beak, a toucan pecks its way into an orange. Fleshy fruits have evolved to attract animals that will spread their seeds. The toucan swallows each mouthful whole, but it digests only the flesh. The seeds pass through its body unharmed, land in its droppings on the ground, and germinate when conditions are right. Fruit-eating birds are useful for plants, because they can scatter seeds far and wide.

Toucan's beak works like pincers to grip fruit

Ripe orange contains pips (seeds)

TYPES OF FLESHY FRUIT

BERRY
There are many different types of fleshy fruit. A berry is a soft fleshy fruit that contains lots of seeds. Berries include currants, gooseberries, grapes, and tomatoes – the biggest-selling fruits in the world. Like many fruits, berries change colour when they are ripe, to show animals that they are ready to eat.

DRUPE
Scientists use the word "drupe" to describe fleshy fruits that have a small number of large, hard seeds, also known as stones. Drupes include cherries, peaches, and apricots, as well as olives and mangoes. When animals eat these fruits, they swallow the juicy flesh, but they usually let the seeds drop to the ground.

AGGREGATE FRUIT
An aggregate fruit – such as a blackberry – is like lots of miniature fruits joined together, and attached to a single stalk. Each miniature fruit develops from a separate ovary and has its own seeds and juicy flesh. Aggregate fruits include all the blackberry's relatives, such as raspberries and loganberries.

FALSE FRUIT
Unlike true fruits, which develop only from a plant's ripened ovary, false fruits develop from the ripened ovary together with other parts of the plant. For example, an apple is made up of the core (which grows from the ovary) and the fleshy part (which grows from a receptacle – the part of the stem directly below the flower).

Love-in-a-mist fruit splits to release seeds

Eryngo flower head produces dozens of small fruits

◀ DRY FRUITS

When people use the word "fruit", they normally mean something soft and juicy that tastes good to eat. But lots of plants, including the ones shown here, have fruits that are hard and dry. Unlike fleshy fruits, dry fruits do not attract animals. Instead, they spread their seeds in other ways. Love-in-the-mist (or nigella) fruits split open when their seeds are ripe, scattering them on the ground. Eryngoes, such as sea holly, have small, dry fruits that develop in a spiky flower head.

SQUIRTING CUCUMBER

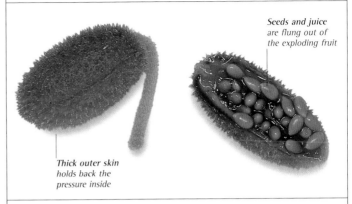

Seeds and juice are flung out of the exploding fruit

Thick outer skin holds back the pressure inside

The squirting cucumber, from southern Europe, has a remarkable way of spreading its seeds. Its fruits are like small, bristly cucumbers. As they ripen, pressure builds up inside them. If anything touches a fruit, it falls from its stalk, explodes, and showers seeds and watery juice up to 3 m (10 ft) away.

Squirting cucumbers are not good at competing with other plants. Their seedlings grow most successfully on bare or recently disturbed ground, such as waste ground, road verges, and pathways. People and dogs on paths help to spread their seeds.

▲ FRUITS THAT SNAP

Many dry fruits snap open or explode when they are ripe, showering seeds a distance away from their parent plant. Pods have two halves that split apart in warm weather – sometimes with a loud, snapping sound. Cranesbills (wild geraniums) have fruits like tiny catapults, which fling their seeds into the air. These fruits all work by drying out. As they dry, tension builds up inside them. Finally, part of the fruit snaps, scattering the seeds.

▲ FLOATING IN THE WIND

Thousands of different plants have dry fruits that float away in the air. Each of the dandelion's fruits has a crown of hairs that works like a parachute and carries a single seed. In dry, breezy weather, the parachute opens and the seed floats away. Some fruits release winged seeds. The largest, found in tropical rainforests, have wings 13 cm (5 in) across, and take several minutes to flutter to the ground.

▲ HITCHING A LIFT

If you go walking in grassy places in summer, you will often find burs hitching a lift on your clothes. These seed heads are actually specialized fruits, armed with spines or hooks. If a person or animal brushes past one, the bur latches on and gets carried away. Later, it drops to the ground and releases its seeds. Most burs are small, but the biggest – from Africa's grasslands – have fearsome hooks over 6 cm (2¼ in) long.

▲ FLOATING FRUITS

Plants that live near rivers or oceans often produce fruits that can float. One of the greatest travelling fruits is the coconut – it can survive for weeks at sea before it gets washed up on a beach. It takes root above the high-tide mark, just beyond the reach of the waves. Floating is a good way of spreading a long distance. It helps to explain why the same seashore plants are often found in many different parts of the world.

◀ TUMBLEWEEDS

Desert plants called tumbleweeds spread their seeds on the move. After flowering, they dry out, curl up into a ball, and their roots break off. The wind can blow tumbleweeds as far as 50 km (31 miles) over open ground, and they pile up against any fences and buildings in their way. Originally from Europe and Asia, they now grow in many parts of the world.

spreading

STARTING LIFE

Every seed contains a tiny embryo plant that is waiting for a chance to grow. If conditions are too dry or too cold, the embryo remains dormant (inactive) – sometimes for many years. As soon as conditions are right, the seed suddenly comes to life. The embryo's cells start dividing, the seed germinates (sprouts), and a new plant starts to take shape. Germination is the most important stage in a plant's life cycle, and it has to run smoothly for the young plant to survive. Once a seed has started germinating, there is no going back – it either succeeds, or it dies.

germination

▼ GERMINATION

Once germination begins, lots of steps happen in quick succession. Like all young plants, this runner bean starts by growing a root, which collects water and anchors it in the soil. Next, it produces a stem, which pushes its way up through the ground. Once it breaks through the surface, its first true leaves open up, allowing the young plant to start making its own food. One week after germinating, the plant is fully self-sufficient and growing fast.

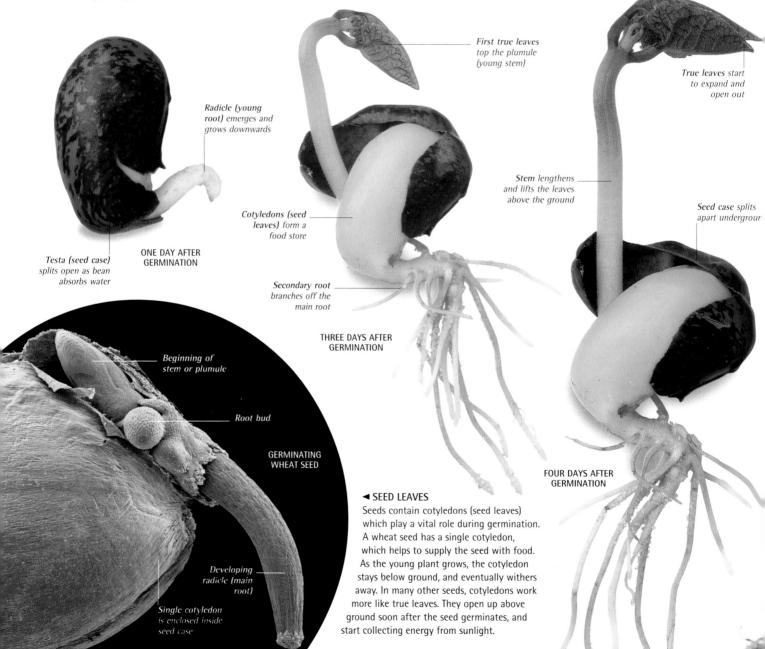

Radicle (young root) emerges and grows downwards

First true leaves top the plumule (young stem)

True leaves start to expand and open out

Cotyledons (seed leaves) form a food store

Stem lengthens and lifts the leaves above the ground

Seed case splits apart undergrour

Testa (seed case) splits open as bean absorbs water

ONE DAY AFTER GERMINATION

Secondary root branches off the main root

THREE DAYS AFTER GERMINATION

Beginning of stem or plumule

Root bud

GERMINATING WHEAT SEED

Developing radicle (main root)

Single cotyledon is enclosed inside seed case

FOUR DAYS AFTER GERMINATION

◄ SEED LEAVES

Seeds contain cotyledons (seed leaves) which play a vital role during germination. A wheat seed has a single cotyledon, which helps to supply the seed with food. As the young plant grows, the cotyledon stays below ground, and eventually withers away. In many other seeds, cotyledons work more like true leaves. They open up above ground soon after the seed germinates, and start collecting energy from sunlight.

Stem continues
growing and
producing
more leaves

FIGHT FOR SURVIVAL ▶
Germinating plants face all kinds of dangers.
A hungry slug can put an end to a young
seedling's chances of survival. Many other
animals, from insects to tiny worms, attack
plants the moment they start to grow. Seedlings
are also attacked by fungi – some kinds can kill
them in just a few hours. To add to their problems,
young plants run the risk of drying out before their
roots have had a chance to develop.

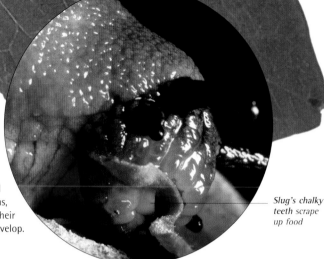

*Slug's chalky
teeth* scrape
up food

▲ SEEDS FROM THE PAST
In the right conditions, seeds can survive
for amazing lengths of time. Lotus seeds
have been known to germinate after
being buried for 1,000 years, while seeds
from these Arctic lupins can survive up
to 10,000 years if they become buried in
frozen soil. Seeds are often preserved in
nature, and scientists are able to use them
to study what kind of plant foods our
ancestors grew and ate.

▲ WAITING FOR FIRE
Bushfires are helpful for many seeds.
Some kinds do not germinate until they
have been brought to life by heat or
sometimes by chemicals in smoke. Fires
clear away dead plants and cover the
ground in a layer of fertile ash where the
young seedlings can take root. Some trees
and bushes, such as conifers and proteas,
wait until fire comes their way before
letting their seeds fall to the ground.

▲ DORMANCY
As long as they stay dry, these beans will
keep for years. Each contains a dormant
embryo, which needs only a tiny amount
of food and moisture to stay alive. In
nature, dormant seeds put up with all
kinds of extreme conditions while they
wait for the right moment to germinate.
Seed dormancy is also useful in the
kitchen, because it enables us to store
seeds without them starting to sprout.

Seed leaves shrink
as their food
reserves are used up

Seed case slowly
rots away

AGAINST THE ODDS ▼
As well as surviving bad weather, pests, and diseases, seedlings have
to cope with competition from other young plants. These beech
seedlings are germinating on a woodland floor, where
they have to compete for light, water, and space.
Nature quickly kills off the weakest seedlings,
so that only the strongest survive. The
odds against survival are huge.
For every million seeds that
beech trees make, less than
10 grow up to be adult,
seed-producing trees.

**ONE WEEK AFTER
GERMINATION**

Network of roots
collects water and
nutrients

SPREADING WITHOUT SEEDS

Many plants can reproduce in two quite different ways. They make seeds, but they also grow parts that can turn into new plants. These new plants often sprout from roots, but they can also grow from stems, buds, or even leaves. This way of spreading is called vegetative reproduction. Unlike sexual reproduction, which works by making seeds, vegetative reproduction always creates young plants that are exactly like their parent. This is very helpful for farmers and gardeners, because it lets them raise identical copies of useful or attractive plants.

▲ PLANT INVADERS
Brambles are particularly good at spreading without seeds. Each long stem arches as it grows, until its tip eventually touches the ground. Then the tip sprouts a cluster of roots to create another plant. Bramble stems can be up to 5 m (16½ ft) long, so plants can spread very quickly if they are not kept in check. They are also good at spreading by seeds, because their sweet blackberries attract many fruit-eating birds.

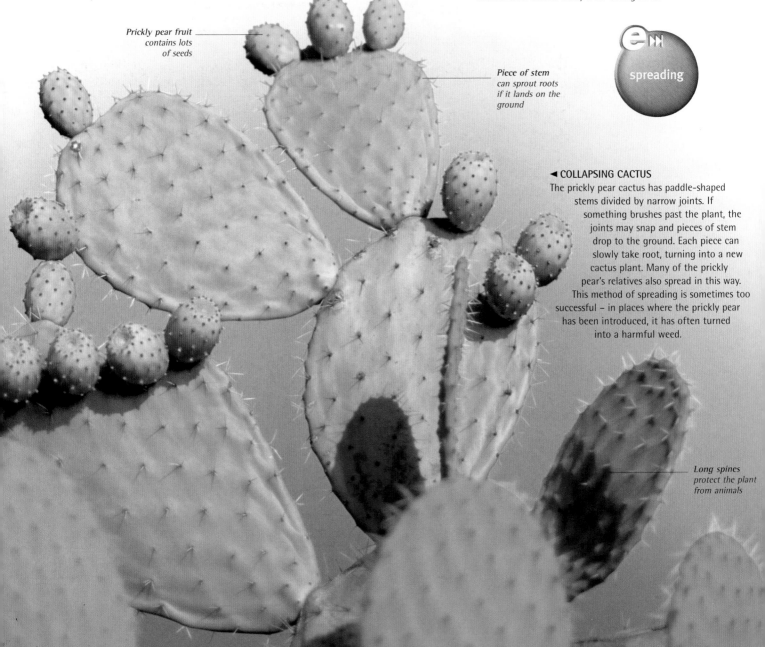

Prickly pear fruit contains lots of seeds

Piece of stem can sprout roots if it lands on the ground

spreading

◄ COLLAPSING CACTUS
The prickly pear cactus has paddle-shaped stems divided by narrow joints. If something brushes past the plant, the joints may snap and pieces of stem drop to the ground. Each piece can slowly take root, turning into a new cactus plant. Many of the prickly pear's relatives also spread in this way. This method of spreading is sometimes too successful – in places where the prickly pear has been introduced, it has often turned into a harmful weed.

Long spines protect the plant from animals

METHODS OF SPREADING

RUNNERS
Strawberries send out stems called runners that snake across the ground and sprout whole new plants. The runners carry food and water from the parent plant to the new plants, until they are big enough to support themselves. Strawberry farmers collect the young plants and use them to start new strawberry beds.

RHIZOMES
Irises grow horizontal stems called rhizomes that grow in the ground or along the surface. As they spread, the rhizomes divide and produce new buds and shoots. Other perennial plants that use rhizomes to reproduce include bamboos, rhubarb, coneflowers, and some troublesome weeds.

BULBS
A bulb is a short, fat bud surrounded by flattened scales. When a bulb grows, it often produces new bulbs, which can break off to form new plants. A bulb of garlic contains lots of these small bulbs (cloves). Bulbs are also underground food stores. Plants can use this food to grow very quickly, flower, and produce seeds.

TUBERS
A tuber is a swollen underground stem. Its main job is to store food, but it can also sprout new plants. Potatoes are tubers. They are covered with small buds called eyes. If a potato is cut up carefully, each eye can become a new plant. Seed potatoes are tubers that have been specially raised for planting, rather than eating.

▼ PLANTS ON LEAVES
The Mexican hat plant has a very unusual way of spreading without making seeds: it grows tiny plantlets along the edges of its leaves. The plantlets gradually drop off, taking root on the ground below. Despite its name, this plant comes from Madagascar, not Mexico. It grows in deserts and dry places and its fleshy leaves store water. The plantlets store water, too, which stops them drying out once they have dropped off the parent plant.

▲ CLUMPS AND CLONES
Plants that spread without seeds often form scattered groups called clones. The biggest clones belong to this North American tree, called the quaking aspen. Some quaking aspen clones spread over 15 hectares (37 acres), and contain thousands of trees connected by a dense network of roots. Like all clones, each one was started by a single parent plant. In the biggest clones, the parent plant started life thousands of years ago.

CUTTINGS

Plant stems often take root if they are cut off and pushed into soil. These young plants, or cuttings, have all been grown in this way. When they grow up, each one will have exactly the same features as its parent plant. In the wild, nature sometimes makes its own cuttings, when parts of plants break off in storms. If rainwater covers the pieces with damp mud, they take root and start to grow. Riverbank trees, such as willows and poplars, often start life in this way.

Fleshy leaf stores water

Plantlet grows on edge of parent plant's leaf

GRASSES

Grasses may not be the world's most colourful plants, but they are some of the most important. There are more than 9,000 different kinds and they grow all over the world, from the tropics to the northern tip of Antarctica. In some habitats, grasses dominate the entire landscape, stretching as far as the eye can see. Grasses are essential food for grazing animals, in the wild and on farms. Cultivated kinds – called cereals – keep the human race alive. Grasses are also good to walk and play on, because they can recover from being mown, scraped, and scuffed.

▼ ANATOMY OF A GRASS
Grass plants have tube-like stems and slender leaves. Each leaf has a sheath that is wrapped around the stem, and a long, flattened blade that ends in a point. Grass flowers are small and inconspicuous, and are pollinated by the wind. The flowers are packed together in flower heads, which look like feathery tufts at the tip of the stems. Grass roots are fibrous and often far-reaching – an important adaptation for life in dry ground.

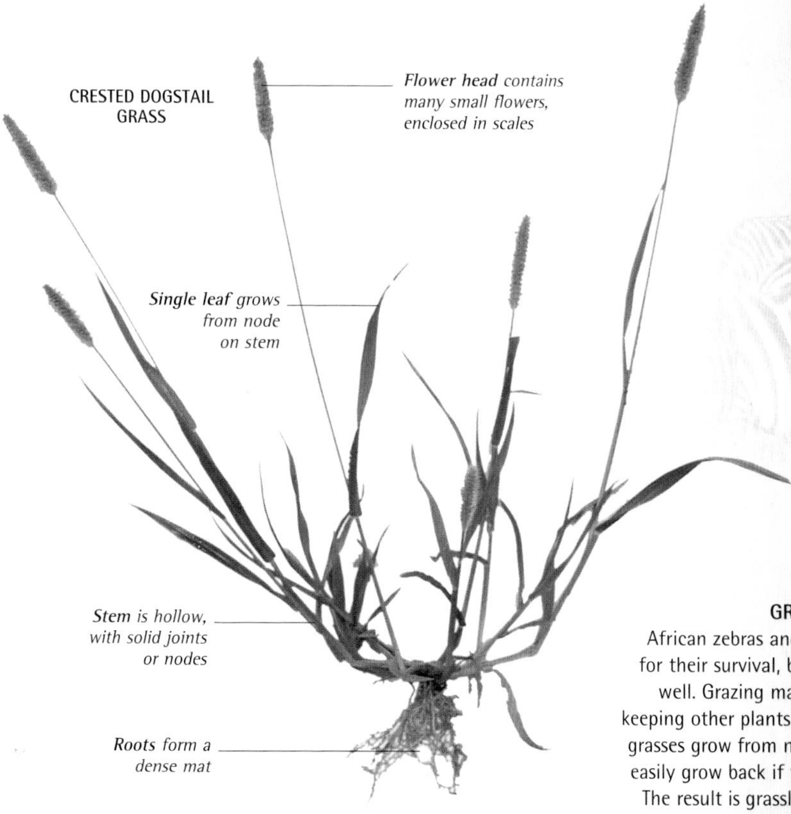

grasses

CRESTED DOGSTAIL GRASS

Flower head contains many small flowers, enclosed in scales

Single leaf grows from node on stem

Stem is hollow, with solid joints or nodes

Roots form a dense mat

GRASSLANDS AND GRAZERS ▲
African zebras and wildebeest depend on grass for their survival, but grass depends on them as well. Grazing mammals help grass to grow by keeping other plants in check. Unlike most plants, grasses grow from near ground level, so they can easily grow back if they are trampled or chewed. The result is grassland – an open habitat where grasses are the dominant plants. Grasslands are most common in dry parts of the world.

HOW A GRASS SPREADS

Marram grass grows among dunes. It spreads by growing horizontal stems called stolons. These push their way through the sand and sprout new plants, even where the sand is several metres deep. Marram grass is a useful plant, because it binds the sand together and stops it blowing inland. Not all grasses grow stolons, and those that do sometimes spread over the surface of the ground, instead of through it.

Bamboo scaffolding bends in the wind so it is suitable even for high-rise buildings

Bamboo poles provide light, strong scaffolding

CONSTRUCTION WORKERS IN HONG KONG

SUGAR CANE ▶

Most of the world's sugar comes from sugar cane – a giant grass that produces large amounts of sweet sap. Sugar is made by cutting down the canes and squeezing out the sap. The sap is boiled until all its water evaporates, leaving sugar crystals behind. Sugar cane is grown in warm parts of the world. Sugar is also produced from sugar beet, a root crop planted in Europe and North America.

BAMBOO ▶

Bamboos are tall grasses with woody stems. Most of them grow in warm regions, although some can survive snow. The largest kinds, from southeast Asia, tower up to 40 m (130 ft) high and have stems thicker than many trees. Bamboos are an important food for animals, including the giant panda. Humans eat bamboo shoots too. Bamboo stems are also used for making furniture, houses, and scaffolding.

Spinifex grass forms a ring

Reed bed grows at the edge of a freshwater lake

Antarctic fur seal comes ashore in October to breed

▲ DESERT GRASSES

Thanks to their narrow leaves and dense roots, grasses are good at withstanding drought. The grass shown here, called spinifex, covers vast areas of the dry Australian outback. Spinifex plants often clump together in rings. This is because the grass keeps spreading outwards, while the centre of the clump slowly dies. Spinifex clumps are an important habitat for animals, including the spinifex pigeon. It nests in the clumps, and feeds on spinifex seeds.

▲ FRESHWATER GRASSES

Many grasses grow in the shallow, fresh water at the edges of streams and lakes. Most of them grow tall so they stand above the water, but some have leaves that flop over its surface. Common reed is one of the most widespread freshwater grasses – it grows in wetlands all over the world. It forms dense reed beds that are important habitats for wildlife, particularly water birds. In winter, its dead stems are sometimes harvested and used for thatching roofs.

▲ TUSSOCK GRASSES

This Antarctic fur seal has come ashore from the chilly Southern Ocean to laze in a bed of tussock grass. This grass lives in cold, windy places, and it forms tall clumps separated by gulleys of waterlogged mud. Few animals can eat it, but it makes a good windbreak. Seals often lie in it when they give birth to their young and it provides a good nesting place for penguins, too. Tussock grass is one of the few flowering plants that survives in Antarctica.

ORCHIDS

With more than 25,000 species, orchids make up one of the largest families of flowering plants. They are found all over the world. In places with temperate climates, they usually grow on the ground, but in the warmth of the tropics, many live high up in trees. Orchids are prized for their flowers, which can last for weeks at a time. Most are pollinated by insects, and a single one can produce more than a million microscopic seeds. Orchid seeds are too small to contain food stores. Instead, they depend on partnerships with fungi to germinate and grow.

Sepal protects the flower while it is still in bud

Colourful lip attracts insects

◀ ORCHID ANATOMY
These eye-catching flowers belong to a hybrid orchid – a kind produced by cross-pollinating different wild species. Like all orchids, its flowers have three outer flaps, or sepals, and three inner ones, or petals. The lowest petal forms a colourful lip, which works like a landing platform for visiting insects. Orchid flowers usually attract insect visitors by being brightly coloured, but some kinds also have a powerful scent.

orchids

▲ POLLINATION AT NIGHT
Most orchid flowers are pollinated by day, but this milky-white species, from the island of Madagascar, is pollinated after dark by moths. Moths visit its flowers to drink their sugary nectar, which is produced at the bottom of a slender tube called a spur. In this orchid, the spurs are up to 30 cm (12 in) long, so only moths with extra-long tongues can reach deep enough to drink. There are many kinds of moth-pollinated orchid, and most have pale flowers that show up well in dim light. Unlike day-pollinated flowers, their perfume smells strongest at night – when moths are on the wing.

INSECT LOOKALIKE

This male bee has been tricked by a remarkable orchid that mimics female bees. To the bee, the bee orchid's flowers not only look like female bees, they smell and feel like them as well. Lured by this mimicry, the male lands on the orchid's flowers and attempts to mate. Before the bee discovers its mistake, the orchid flower fastens a package of pollen to its body. The bee flies off, and delivers the pollen to the next bee orchid flower that it visits.

▲ TERRESTRIAL ORCHID
The lady's slipper orchid, from northern Europe, is a terrestrial species, which means that it grows in the ground. Like all terrestrial orchids, it has thickened roots that store food underground. It is pollinated by small bees, and it gets its name from the shape of its flowers. Slipper orchids are becoming rare because they are often dug up or picked.

▲ SAPROPHYTIC ORCHID
The coral-root orchid grows in the ground but, unlike most plants, it does not have any leaves. This means it cannot photosynthesize (use the energy in sunshine to make food and grow). Instead, the plant works together with underground fungi to feed on dead matter in the soil. Orchids like this are called saprophytes. They spend most of their lives hidden, only appearing above the surface when they flower.

▲ EPIPHYTIC ORCHID
In tropical rainforests, orchids often grow high up in trees, where they have a better chance of soaking up the sunshine. Know as epiphytes, these orchids have specialized roots that anchor them to branches and that collect moisture from rain. Their roots often gather fallen leaves or bark pieces, creating mini compost heaps that help them to grow.

◄ BREEDING ORCHIDS
Laid out in neat rows, these glass dishes contain small pieces of orchid stem that will grow into whole new plants. Orchids are difficult to raise from seed, because they depend on special fungi for their survival, and take a long time to grow. This way of propagating orchids, called meristem culture, is much quicker.

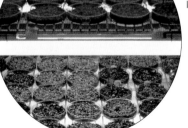

Vanilla pod contains tiny, black seeds

▲ ORCHID NURSERY
Working in a specially shaded greenhouse, a nurseryman waters tropical orchids that are being grown for sale. Orchids are popular house plants because of their showy, long-lasting flowers. Terrestrial orchids are raised in pots of soil, but epiphytic orchids are grown in pots of bark chips. A daily shower of water re-creates the conditions of their rainforest home.

VANILLA PODS ►
Only one orchid species – vanilla – is cultivated as a crop. Vanilla pods have a pleasant perfume that is used to flavour ice cream, chocolate, and other foods. The vanilla orchid was first used by the Aztecs of Mexico. Today, most vanilla is grown in Madagascar.

BROAD-LEAVED TREES

Broad-leaved trees are flowering plants. There are at least 25,000 kinds, including more than 1,000 kinds of acacia and 600 different oaks. Some broad-leaved trees are evergreen, but many lose their leaves in the winter or when the weather turns hot and dry. Broad-leaved trees are extremely important for animals (they supply shelter and food) and for humans (they supply timber, fruit, spices, medicinal drugs, and many other plant products).

HIMALAYAN BIRCH

SWEET BUCKEYE

BUR OAK

PECAN

MAGNOLIA

SILK TREE

ANATOMY OF A TREE ▶
This maple is a typical broad-leaved tree. It has a pillar-like trunk, and its spreading branches form a rounded crown. It looks quite different to typical conifers, which are tall and straight. The maple's dangly flowers are yellowish-green, and are pollinated by the wind. The female flowers produce fruits called samara, made up of a pair of seeds attached to two papery wings. A large tree like this can make thousands of samara each year.

◀ LEAVES
The leaves of broad-leaved trees vary enormously. Some are as small as a fingernail, but the largest are up to 20 m (66 ft) long. Broad-leaves can have a simple shape, without any divisions or lobes, or they can be divided into leaflets, all attached to the same leaf stalk. Some broad-leaved trees, such as eucalyptuses, have one type of leaf when they are young, and another when they are mature.

broad leaves

Leaves appear as the flowers fade

MAPLE TREE IN SUMMER

Sapwood conducts water

Bark

Phloem

Cambium contains active, dividing cells

Heartwood is all dead cells

▲ WOOD
A tree's trunk and branches are built in the same way. On the outside is a protective layer of bark. Beneath the bark, a layer called the phloem carries the tree's sap. Next is the cambium – a thin layer of cells that constantly divide to thicken the trunk or branch. The sapwood contains xylem cells, which carry water up from the roots. Dead heartwood gives the tree extra strength and is found in the middle of the trunk and oldest branches.

TYPES OF BARK

CORK OAK
This evergreen oak tree has thick bark with deep furrows and ridges. The bark can be stripped away in curved sheets, and used for making cork. If this is done carefully, a new layer of smooth bark slowly forms in its place. Cork can be harvested from the same tree for over a century without doing the tree any harm.

LONDON PLANE
Found in cities, the London plane has pale grey bark, which peels away in large flakes to reveal patches of creamy new bark underneath. Trees take in air through small pores in their bark, and the plane tree's peeling flakes help to stop its pores clogging up. This makes it good at surviving in polluted city air.

PAPER BIRCH
Birch trees have paper-thin, pale-coloured bark. It peels off in flakes or strips as the tree's trunk grows wider. Bark from the paper birch is waterproof. Native Americans once used it to make canoes and to build wigwam roofs. In Central Asia, Buddhist monks used a similar kind of bark to write on, more than 2,000 years ago.

Prickly case protects nuts while they develop

Up to three nuts develop in the case

Buds at ends of twigs will sprout next year's flowers

MAPLE TREE IN WINTER

▲ FLOWERS

All broad-leaved trees have flowers. These flowers belong to a crab apple – a small ornamental tree that is often grown in gardens. It is pollinated by bees, which are attracted by the colour and scent of the flowers. Some tropical trees, such as the jacaranda, are even more spectacular, because they often flower when they have no leaves. Wind-pollinated trees, such as maples, are quite different. Even when they are in full bloom, their small, green flowers can be hard to see.

▲ SEEDS AND FRUIT

When broad-leaved trees have finished flowering, they produce their fruit and seeds. These seeds are sweet chestnuts, which grow inside a prickly case. The case falls to the ground when the nuts (seeds) are ripe, then splits open to release them. Many broad-leaved trees grow fleshy fruit, which have evolved to attract animals. One of the biggest kinds, called the jackfruit, comes from southeast Asia. The fruit tastes like a cross between a pineapple and a banana, and can weigh up to 35 kg (77 lb).

◄ EVERGREEN TREES

Evergreen trees keep their leaves all year round. Each leaf often lasts for several years, falling only when another one is ready to take its place. Nearly all conifers are evergreen, and so are most broad-leaved trees that grow in rainforests, or in places where winters are mild. Evergreen leaves are usually thicker and tougher than deciduous ones, because they are built to last. Some kinds – such as eucalyptus leaves – contain strong-tasting oils. These help to protect them from insects and other leaf-eating animals.

▲ DECIDUOUS TREES

Like this maple, most deciduous trees lose all their leaves in autumn and grow a complete new set in spring. This saves energy, because the trees can shut down until good growing conditions return. In the tropics, where the year is alternately wet and dry, broad-leaved trees often lose their leaves as the dry weather begins. They grow a new set when the rains return.

AUTUMN COLOURS ►

Like many deciduous trees, these maples in New England, northeastern USA, blaze with colour in autumn. Just before it drops its leaves, a tree takes back the chlorophyll that makes its leaves green. The tree will reuse it in next year's leaves. Without the chlorophyll, pigments that were previously hidden are revealed. Autumn colours are brightest in places where warm summers are followed by cold autumn nights.

Maple leaves turn red, yellow, and orange in autumn

PALMS

With their slender trunks and elegant leaves, palms look quite different to other broad-leaved trees. There are more than 3,000 kinds and almost all of them live in warm parts of the world. Some palms grow low to the ground, but the tallest kinds tower over 40 m (130 ft) high. Their leaves are tough, long-lasting, and may be metres long. Palms are important for wildlife. Birds nest among their leaves, and their fruit is eaten by all sorts of animals, from monkeys to robber crabs. People cultivate palms for their fruit, too.

Roots often sprout from above ground level

Leaf lasts for several years

Wood is light and fibrous, without any growth rings

◄ PROFILE OF A PALM
Like nearly all palm trees, these coconut palms have a single trunk without any branches. The trunk is topped by a tuft of large leaves, which grow one by one from a central bud. This bud is vital to the palm – if it is cut off or killed by cold, the tree stops growing and dies. A palm's flowers and fruit usually grow in clusters at the base of its leaves. When these coconuts are ripe, they will fall and float away in the sea.

FAN-SHAPED
PALM LEAF

FEATHER-SHAPED
PALM LEAF

◄ PALM LEAVES
Compared to other trees, palms have very large leaves. The record is 20 m (66 ft) long, but even small palms can have leaves more than 5 m (16½ ft) long. Palm leaves are stiff and often spiky. They are usually divided up into lots of leaflets, attached to a central stem. In some palms, the leaflets spread in a semicircle, making a shape like a fan. In others, they form two ranks, making a shape like a feather.

PALM HABITATS

NYPA PALMS IN WETLAND

Palms all need warmth, but they live in a variety of habitats. Some, like the nypa palm, grow in tropical wetlands and need lots of moisture. Nypa palms form clumps on the edges of rivers and lakes.

Palms also grow in tropical rainforests. Many rainforest palms are small, with thin stems. Others, such as rattans, grow long, flexible trunks that sprawl over neighbouring trees.

DATE PALMS IN DESERT

Palm trees also thrive in deserts, a habitat in which few other trees survive. They often spring up along dry riverbeds, where their roots tap into water that is hidden underground.

HOW PALMS GROW

YOUNG PALM
This coconut palm has started growing after being washed up on a beach. Like all palms, it produces a tuft of leaves on a slender trunk. The base of each leaf wraps around the trunk, and as each leaf emerges, the young palm gets slightly taller. Meanwhile, it grows lots of roots to anchor itself in the shifting sand.

MIDDLE AGE
As the palm gets older, the tuft of leaves grows higher and forms the tree's trunk. The palm's trunk gets longer, but it does not get any thicker. This is because its wood stops growing once it has been formed. Unlike most trees, the palm does not have true bark, and its trunk cannot repair any cuts or damage.

MATURITY
The palm is now 10 years old. It has adult-sized leaves and its trunk is about 8 m (26 ft) high. It is fully mature, and has started to produce flowers and fruits. Some palm trees flower in particular seasons, but coconut palms can flower all year round. The palm will keep growing as long as its central bud stays alive.

◄ PALM FRUIT

This plantation worker is carrying fruits from an oil palm – a tree that is widely grown in warm parts of the world. Like most palm fruits, each one contains a single seed. The oil from these fruits is used in a variety of products, from detergents to processed food. Many palms, including the oil palm and coconut palm, have fruits with hard husks or shells. The date palm is very different. Its fruits, called dates, have an outer layer of sweet-tasting flesh.

PALM PRODUCTS

Palm trees are used in an extraordinary number of different ways. They provide food, and also sap that can be used for making drinks. Palm sap is sometimes fermented to make palm wine.

Some palms are an important source of fibres, such as raffia and coir. Raffia comes from the leaves of the raffia palm, and is used for basketwork and weaving. Coir comes from the outer husks of coconuts, and is used in brushes, matting, and ropes.

Palm leaves can be used to make thatched roofs and beach umbrellas. Stem wood is sometimes used for building or fence posts. Palm trees also produce useful waxes.

CLIMBING PALMS ►

Rattans and their relatives have extremely slender trunks, but they grow up to 150 m (492 ft) long by flopping over other trees. These palms live in the rainforests of southeast Asia, and they scramble up neighbouring trees to get a share of the light. Their trunks have backward-pointing spines, which help them to hook over branches, and then stay in place. Rattan trunks are often harvested and used to make furniture, because they are strong but easy to bend.

Dense cluster of leaves is supported by barrel-shaped trunk

Older leaf is away from the centre of the fan

Young leaf sprouts in the centre of the fan

palms

Leaf at fan's base will soon drop off

▲ ENDANGERED PALMS

Over 10 per cent of the world's palms are threatened with extinction. This Chilean wine palm has become rare because its sap is used to make wine. To collect the sap, the top of the trunk is cut off and this kills the tree. This species is now protected, but many other palms are in danger because their habitats are being destroyed. This kind of threat is much more difficult to stop.

TRAVELLER'S TREE ▲

When fully grown, the traveller's tree has gigantic leaves that form a fan shape that may be 8 m (26 ft) across. Originally from Madagascar, it is now grown in parks and gardens in warm parts of the world. The traveller's tree is not a palm, but it belongs to the same group of flowering plants (monocots) and it grows in a palm-like way. Other palm-like plants include bananas and screw pines, which grow on tropical shores.

CARNIVOROUS PLANTS

Plants do not need food, but they do need mineral nutrients (nitrogen) to grow. Most plants absorb enough nitrogen from nitrates in the soil, but carnivorous (meat-eating) plants get theirs by catching small animals, and by digesting their dead remains. Insects make up most of their victims, but some kinds of carnivorous plant can trap larger prey such as centipedes and frogs. Carnivorous plants live all over the world in habitats where the soil is boggy and poor, and where nitrates are in short supply. To capture their victims, these plants use special traps, which often take the place of normal leaves.

e ▸▸
carnivores

RAINFOREST TRAP ▶
Tropical pitcher plants have jug-shaped traps on the ends of their leaves. Each trap has a lid to keep off the rain and a wide, slippery rim. The rim produces nectar, and insects land on it looking for a meal. Once an insect has touched down, it loses its footing and drops into a pool of fluid where it drowns. Over the next few days, enzymes in the fluid gradually digest the remains of the dead insect. The smallest pitchers are no bigger than a thimble and grow at ground level. The largest can hold over 1 litre (35 fl oz) of liquid, and are produced by evergreen climbers. Tropical pitcher plants grow in forests and wet grasslands, in Madagascar, southern Asia, and Australia.

Pitcher is red and yellow to attract insects

Twining tendril can wrap around other plants for support

VENUS FLYTRAP

LANDING PAD
The Venus flytrap has spring-loaded leaves that can snap shut to trap insects. Here, a damselfly has landed on one of the plant's traps. The trap has two pads joined by a hinge, and each pad has a fringe of stiff spikes. Three small bristles, in the middle of each pad, work like a set of triggers to activate the trap.

THE TRAP CLOSES
If the damselfly touches two of the triggers at the same time, the trap springs into action. The hinge closes and the pads snap together. As this happens, the spikes around the lobes mesh together like fingers, making it very hard for the damselfly to escape. In less than a second, the insect will be completely trapped.

DIGESTING THE PREY
Once the trap has closed, the pads start to produce digestive enzymes. These break down the damselfly's body, releasing nutrients that the plant can absorb. After about a week, the trap opens again, letting the dead remains fall to the ground. Each trap digests about two or three meals, and then withers away.

Lid stops
rainwater diluting
the digestive fluid

Slippery rim
produces nectar to
attract insect prey

Crab spider has
adapted to hunt
on pitcher's rim

Giant hissing
cockroach slips
into the trap

Presence of
insects triggers
digestive glands to
release enzymes

Pitcher pool
contains enzymes
that break down
nutrients from
insect prey

Undigested insect
body part sinks to
the bottom of the
pitcher

SUNDEWS ▶

Carnivorous bog plants called sundews are covered with sticky hairs. At the tip of each hair is a bead of glue, which looks like a drop of dew. If an insect mistakes the glistening droplet for nectar and lands, it is immediately stuck fast. Nearby hairs slowly fold over the insect, and then digest it on the spot. There are more than 100 kinds of sundew. They grow all over the world, on moorlands and mountains, and in other places where the soil is wet and acidic.

BUTTERWORTS ▶

The butterwort's leaves are covered in two kinds of gland. One produces a glue that traps any insect that lands on the leaf. The other produces digestive juices. The plant's name comes from the belief that the juices can turn milk into butter. Many carnivorous plants have pale flowers, but the butterwort's are bright blue. There are about 40 kinds of butterwort. Native to bogs, they are sometimes grown in greenhouses to keep small insect pests under control.

SARRACENIAS ▶

North American pitcher plants (sarracenias) have a cluster of pitchers that sprout from the ground. Their pitchers are shaped like ice-cream cones, and they can be up to 90 cm (35½ in) high. Like tropical pitchers, they have a lid that keeps out the rain, and they give off a strong smell that attracts flies and other insects that breed in rotting remains. Sarracenias grow in boggy places all over the continent, from Florida in the south up to the Canadian Arctic.

BLADDERWORTS ▶

The only carnivorous plants that trap animals underwater are bladderworts. They float on the surface and have trailing, underwater leaves that are armed with tiny, bubble-shaped traps. The traps are triggered by small bristles, which are attached to a hinged door. If an animal touches one of these bristles, the trap suddenly opens up, sucking the animal inside. Here, a water flea is swimming close to a trap that has already caught a meal.

EPIPHYTES

Instead of growing on the ground, epiphytes perch high up on trees and other plants. This gives them a good share of the sunlight, without having to grow tall themselves. Most epiphytes use their roots to stay in place, and they get all the water they need from rain. They collect mineral nutrients from airborne dust or from dead leaves that drop onto them from above. Epiphytes include liverworts, mosses, and ferns, as well as lichens and many kinds of flowering plant. They are most common in tropical rainforests, but can also grow in cool, damp woodlands.

GARDENS IN THE SKY ▶
This tropical tree trunk is smothered with epiphytes and climbing plants. The climbers are rooted in the soil, but the epiphytes spend their whole lives off the ground. Some epiphytes grow on vertical tree trunks, while others cling to sloping branches. Unlike parasitic plants, epiphytes do not steal water or nutrients from their hosts. Most epiphytes have tiny, wind-borne seeds or spores that drift from tree to tree.

Flower produces nectar to attract hummingbirds

epiphytes

Tree frog has sticky toe pads that can cling to leaves

◀ BROMELIAD
Tropical plants called bromeliads include some of the world's biggest epiphytes. This one, from South America, has eye-catching flowers that are pollinated by hummingbirds. Like many bromeliads, it uses its leaves to channel rainwater towards a tank-like hollow at the centre of the plant. Bromeliad tanks are important habitats. Some tree frogs even lay their eggs in them and their tadpoles develop there, high above the ground.

EPIPHYTES IN COOL CLIMATES

These gnarled oak trees are covered in mosses, some of the commonest epiphytes in places that are cool and damp. Mosses grow well on oaks, because oak bark has lots of crevices where moss spores can start to grow.

Lichens are another kind of epiphyte that grows on temperate trees. Some lichens grow flat on tree trunks, while others look like tiny bushes, sprouting from branches and twigs.

STAYING IN PLACE ▶

To survive, epiphytes need to cling on tight. Epiphytic orchids do this with special roots that wrap around branches. These roots have a spongy covering, and they absorb water and nutrients when it rains. Over half the world's orchids are epiphytic, and many of them live in tropical rainforests, where it is always warm and wet. Their seeds are microscopic, and they spread through the forest canopy on the slightest breeze.

Green root tip carries out photosynthesis

▲ EPIPHYLLS

This liverwort is growing over the surface of a single leaf. Plants that live like this are called epiphylls, and most of them are found in tropical rainforests. Epiphylls usually grow on large evergreen leaves, in the damp shade near the forest floor. As well as liverworts, epiphylls also include mosses and algae. Together, they can completely cover a leaf, weighing it down and soaking up most of its light.

▲ SPANISH MOSS

In the southeastern United States, Spanish moss trails gracefully from the branches of many trees. Despite its name, this epiphyte is not a true moss, but a bromeliad. Most bromeliads have fleshy leaves, but Spanish moss has hanging stems, covered with tiny scales that collect moisture. The stems of Spanish moss can grow over 1 m (3¼ ft) long. Like all bromeliads, it grows in tropical parts of the Americas, but not in any other part of the world.

▲ AIR PLANTS

With their strange shapes and even stranger lifestyles, air plants are often grown as house plants. Unlike most epiphytes, they can live in dry habitats, and they cling to other plants not only with their roots, but also with their snaking leaves. Air plants normally grow on shrubs and trees, but may also set up home on artificial structures such as television aerials and telephone wires. Close relatives of Spanish moss, they have leaves covered with water-collecting scales.

CREEPERS AND CLIMBERS

Plants need light. To get enough, most grow strong stems that can carry lots of leaves. Creepers and climbing plants are different. Instead of supporting themselves, they cling to nearby objects. Many of them climb up other plants, but some scramble up rocks, fences, and buildings in their search for a share of the sunshine. This way of life has one big advantage – creepers and climbing plants do not need strong stems, so they have more energy for growing very quickly. Creepers and climbers come from many different families of plant, and have developed lots of ways of getting a grip.

SWISS CHEESE PLANT ▶
Popular as a house plant, the Swiss cheese plant (or monstera) is a climber that grows wild in the rainforests of Central America. As a seedling, the Swiss cheese plant grows across the forest floor, heading towards the shade. This helps it to find a tree trunk, which it can climb up towards the light. As it grows, the plant produces lots of slender roots, which hold it to the tree trunk like pieces of rope. Its leaves also become much bigger and develop holes so they look like slices of Swiss cheese. When the plant is fully grown, it may be up to 20 m (66 ft) high. If its host tree turns out to be too short, the plant uses a special survival tactic to reach the light. It grows back down to the ground and seeks out another tree trunk, before starting its climb again.

creepers

◀ LIANAS
Lianas are large, twining plants which have thick, woody stems. They grow in tropical forests, and they use other plants to get a foothold in the canopy – the highest level of branches and leaves in the forest. Lianas often outlive the plants that they grow up, which leaves their stems trailing through the air. Some lianas can be over 100 m (328 ft) long, with stems over 50 cm (20 in) thick. In the canopy, their leaves can be sprawled over an area as big as a football pitch.

HOLDING ON

Tendril may have up to a dozen pads

▲ TWINING CLIMBERS

Morning-glory or ipomoea is a typical climber, which grows by twining around other plants. Its stems turn in tight spirals, which gives them a tight grip. Twining plants always turn in one direction. Seen from above, morning-glories twine in an anticlockwise spiral. When twining plants germinate, their growing stems often sweep around in circles, close to the ground. This gives them the best chance of finding something that they can climb.

▲ CLINGING ROOTS

Ivy clings to trees and walls using small roots that grow along its stems. The roots grow into crevices in bark or brickwork. When an ivy plant is mature, its top grows out to form a bush, sometimes high above the ground. Ivy is not a parasite because it does not steal water or food, but it can kill trees by smothering their leaves. Ivy can also be a problem on old buildings. If the plant is pulled off, pieces of brick and mortar often come away with it.

▲ STICKY PADS

Virginia creepers can climb up almost any surface, thanks to their sucker-like pads. These develop at the end of small tendrils, which spread out like the fingers of a hand. As each pad grows, it presses into the smallest cracks and crevices to obtain an extremely firm grip. The tendrils then tighten up to pull the plant close to its support. Virginia creepers are popular garden plants, because they turn a colourful, bright red in the autumn.

Tendril makes contact and its tip starts to curl

Base of tendril coils up to strengthen its hold

◀ TENDRILS

Many climbing plants stay in place by using slender threads called tendrils, which have touch-sensitive tips. Below, a tendril of white bryony is curling around a grape hyacinth – but any solid object would do. Once a tendril has got a good grip, its base starts to coil up like a spring. This tightens up the tendril, helping the plant to stay in place. Because the tendrils have this spring at their base, they are more flexible and do not snap when the plant blows about in the wind. Tendrils are very sensitive to touch. If they are stroked with a pencil, they can start curling in less than five minutes.

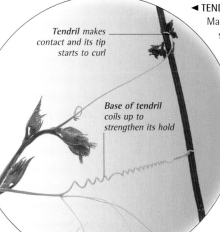

▲ RAMBLERS AND SCRAMBLERS

This rose plant has grown through a bush. Instead of hanging on tightly, it leans against other plants, and uses its thorns to stay in place. Plants that do this can reach impressive sizes. The world's largest rambling rose bush has a trunk that is 1 m (3¼ ft) thick, and it covers an area as big as an Olympic swimming pool. Scrambling plants grow in the same way, but nearer the ground. Their flexible stems sprawl over anything in their path, including rocks and other plants.

PARASITIC PLANTS

Instead of growing on their own, parasitic plants live by stealing from other plants, known as their hosts. Total parasites do not have leaves and they steal everything that they need to survive. Hemiparasites have leaves and can make their own food, but they steal the water and nutrients they need to grow. Parasitic plants grow in many habitats, from rainforests to farmland. Most are easy to spot, but some live hidden inside their hosts or underground. These parasites are only visible for a short time each year, when they burst into flower.

CROP PARASITES

There are more than 100 kinds of broomrape (top) and they cause serious damage to crops, particularly peas and beans. They break into crops from underground and are total parasites, relying on their hosts for everything. They produce brownish or yellowish flowers.

Witchweed (bottom) is a parasite from Asia and Africa that attacks maize and other cereals. Like broomrape, it depends completely on its hosts, and it attacks them underground. Witchweed is easy to spot because it has colourful flowers.

Getting rid of crop parasites is not easy. The only sure method is to switch to a different crop plant that the parasite cannot attack.

GIANT PARASITE ▼

Rafflesia, a parasitic plant from southeast Asia, produces the world's biggest flowers. It grows in rainforests, and spends most of its life hidden inside climbing vines. Each of its rubbery blooms is up to 90 cm (3 ft) across, and has an overpowering smell that attracts swarms of flies. Rafflesia flowers produce squashy fruits the size of tennis balls. These stick to the feet of forest elephants, which spread the rafflesia seeds to other vines.

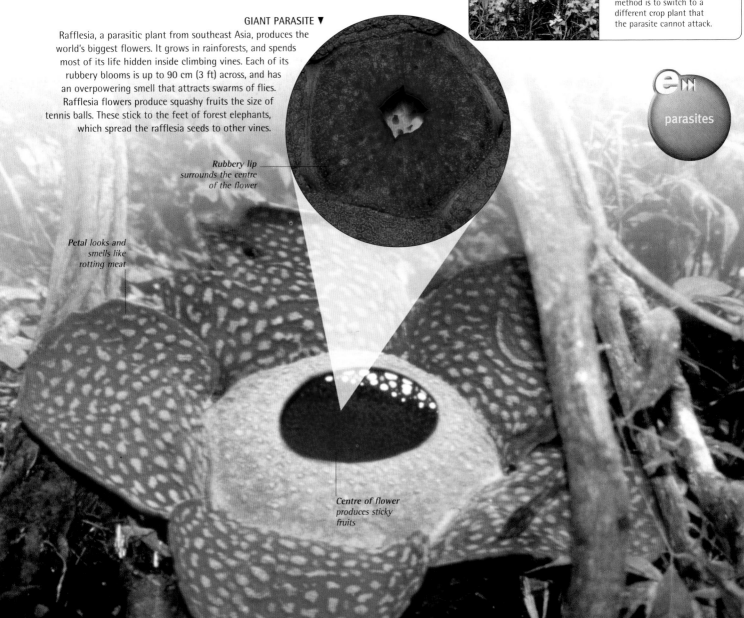

Rubbery lip surrounds the centre of the flower

Petal looks and smells like rotting meat

Centre of flower produces sticky fruits

parasites

DODDER

SMOTHERED
This bush is festooned with dodder, a total parasite that looks like spaghetti. Dodder germinates in the soil, but its roots shrivel up once it starts climbing its host. Dodder grows swellings called haustoria, which break into the host to steal food and water. There are over 100 types of dodder and they attack many kinds of plant.

DODDER FLOWERS
Dodder plants grow clusters of tiny pink or white flowers. These are often pollinated by flies and they produce minute seeds that drop onto the ground. When a dodder seed germinates, the young plant grows a long stem that reaches out to find a host. If it does not find a host plant quickly, the dodder dies.

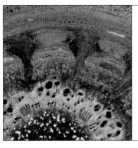

BREAKING IN
This view through a microscope shows a dodder stem coloured orange and its haustoria dark green. The host plant's stem is coloured turquoise. The haustoria force their way into the host's stem and connect with pipelines that carry food and water (shown in pink). Sometimes the parasite steals so much that it kills its host.

Brilliant yellow flowers produce lots of nectar

Thrush spreads mistletoe by carrying its berries from tree to tree

MISTLETOE ►
Mistletoes are parasites that grow on trees. They get water and minerals from their host tree, but they have their own leaves and they make food for themselves. To spread, mistletoe has to scatter its seeds so that they reach other trees. Common mistletoe does this by making sticky berries. These are carried away by birds, which wipe them on a branch to get rid of their sticky coating. When they do this, the seeds stick to the branch and start to grow.

Green leaves enable mistletoe to make food through photosynthesis

Mistletoe grows into host branch

▲ PARASITIC TREE
The Australian Christmas tree is one of the world's most spectacular parasitic plants. When it comes into flower, in December, it is covered with yellow blooms. This eye-catching tree is a hemiparasite, collecting water and nutrients from grass plants growing nearby. By tapping into all of their roots, the tree is able to collect far more water than if it used roots of its own. The Australian Christmas tree belongs to the same family of plants as mistletoes.

PLANT DEFENCES

From the moment plants start life, they have to fend off hungry animals. Insects suck their sap, nibble their leaves, or burrow through their stems. Much larger plant-eaters, such as deer, strip off mouthfuls of bark and foliage, or uproot plants and swallow them whole. Plants cannot run away, so they use special defences that keep these intruders at bay. Some plants defend themselves by being difficult to get at or painful to eat. Others taste bad or are even poisonous, so that animals learn to leave them alone.

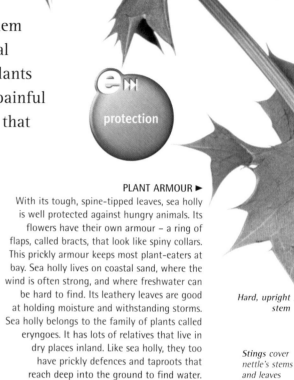

Stiff bracts grow under each flower head

Spiky leaf

protection

PLANT ARMOUR ▶
With its tough, spine-tipped leaves, sea holly is well protected against hungry animals. Its flowers have their own armour – a ring of flaps, called bracts, that look like spiny collars. This prickly armour keeps most plant-eaters at bay. Sea holly lives on coastal sand, where the wind is often strong, and where freshwater can be hard to find. Its leathery leaves are good at holding moisture and withstanding storms. Sea holly belongs to the family of plants called eryngoes. It has lots of relatives that live in dry places inland. Like sea holly, they too have prickly defences and taproots that reach deep into the ground to find water.

Hard, upright stem

Stings cover nettle's stems and leaves

▲ DEFENSIVE HAIRS
Lamb's ears is a herb with soft, silky leaves that are covered with tiny hairs. The hairs help to keep the leaves cool, by shading them from the sun. They also get in the way of small insects that might want to eat the leaves. Plant hairs sometimes have branches, creating a tangled, felty layer that is almost impossible for insects to penetrate. In many plants, the hairs also produce blobs of glue, which give the leaf even more protection.

Cap contains poison

Sharp hair is made of silica

Peacock caterpillar avoids stings as it feeds

◀ NETTLES
Stinging nettles are covered with sharp hairs that contain tiny doses of poison. Each hair is hollow and ends in a hard cap. If an animal brushes the hair, the cap breaks off and the poison is jabbed into the animal's skin. Grazing mammals soon learn not to eat nettles. Tree nettles, from Australia and New Zealand, are particularly poisonous and can even kill animals that come into contact with them.

▲ OVERCOMING PLANT DEFENCES
Despite their stings, nettles are not completely safe from attack. Many caterpillars feed on nettles. Newly hatched caterpillars are small enough to move around the stinging hairs, while adult caterpillars are too light and too slow-moving to snap off the hair tips. Most caterpillars feed for about four weeks before they turn into a butterfly. Nettles are a good source of food, because their leaves are rich in nutrients, and the stings prevent competition from bigger plant-eaters.

Cluster of small flowers

Swelling forms at the base of the tree's thorns

Ant enters and leaves swelling through tiny holes

▼ANIMAL ALLIES

In the battle to ward off animals, some plants use other animals to help them. The whistling thorn tree, from Central America, has hollow swellings at the base of its thorns. Ants live in these swellings. If any animal tries to eat the tree's leaves, the ants attack it. On windy days, the swellings sometimes makes a whistling sound, which is how the tree gets its name.

Single crystal of calcium oxalate

Cells from the centre of the leaf

▲ CHEMICAL DEFENCES

This plant, called dumb-cane, has crystals of calcium oxalate in its leaves. The sharp crystals stick in animals' throats and make them choke. Altogether, plants use thousands of different chemicals for self-defence. Some, such as tannins, simply make a plant taste bad. Others, such as cyanide and strychnine, are extremely poisonous even in small amounts.

▲ LATEX

Spurges, such as this fireglow spurge, ooze a milky fluid called latex if their stems are broken. Latex has a strong, peppery taste. It makes stems and leaves unpleasant or even dangerous for animals to eat. Latex also seals cuts, so fungi cannot get in. Rubber trees belong to the spurge family. Natural rubber is collected by scoring the bark of the trees, so that their latex oozes out.

▲ CAMOUFLAGE

Living stones grow in the deserts of southern Africa. They have two fleshy, mottled leaves that make them look just like small pebbles. Their camouflage is almost perfect – until the time comes for them to flower. Camouflage is much rarer in plants than in animals. One reason is that plant-eating animals usually find their food by its smell, not by its appearance.

POISONOUS PLANTS

Plants produce thousands of different substances as they develop. Most of these substances are harmless, but some are poisonous. Ricin, from the beans of the castor-oil plant, is one of the most powerful poisons in the world. Cyanide from laurel leaves can kill living cells in minutes, while alkaloids from nightshades can paralyze muscles and make breathing difficult. Such poisons are useful to plants, because they protect them from hungry animals. Plant poisons usually work when they are swallowed, but some are harmful even if they are touched.

▲ LONG-LASTING POISON
Poison ivy is one of the most dangerous plants in North America. It contains urushiol, a thick, sticky poison that causes severe swelling if it touches bare skin. The poison can stay active for months if it has been accidentally wiped onto clothes or shoes. If a poison ivy plant is burned, it produces poisonous smoke. Despite its name, poison ivy is not a true ivy, although it does sometimes climb up tree trunks. Its leaves have three shiny leaflets, which turn bright red before they fall in autumn.

THE WORLD'S DEADLIEST PLANT ▶
The castor-oil plant produces the deadliest poison in the living world. The poison, a protein called ricin, is found only in its bean-shaped seeds. Ricin is 10,000 times more deadly than rattlesnake venom and there is no known antidote. In 1978, it was used in a famous assassination, when a Bulgarian journalist called Georgy Markov was stabbed in the leg by an umbrella. After he died, doctors found a ricin-dipped pellet, smaller than a grain of rice, in Markov's leg. Ricin is removed as a waste product when castor-oil seeds are pressed for their oil. Castor oil is an extremely versatile oil that is used in medicines, perfumes, soaps, plastics, and paints.

Castor-oil seed contains deadly ricin

poisonous plants

Milkweed leaf contains poisons called cardiac glycosides

Small fruit turns black when ripe

Cherry laurel leaf gives off cyanide when damaged

▲ POISONOUS LEAVES
Cherry laurel is a fast-growing garden shrub. Its thick, evergreen leaves are well protected from insects, because they give off cyanide if they are pierced or crushed. Cyanide is poisonous to plants, so the cherry laurel stores the ingredients needed to make cyanide, instead of cyanide itself. If an insect bites into a cherry laurel leaf, the ingredients mix together. This releases cyanide, which either kills the insect or makes it move to another plant.

POISONS IN THE SEA

Some algae produce poisons that are just as deadly as ones from plants. This picture shows a red tide, which is produced by millions of drifting algae called dinoflagellates. The algae release poisons as they grow, killing fish and other animals.

Red tides usually occur in warm parts of the world, in water that contains lots of nutrients, including fertilizers or sewage. After a severe red tide, thousands of dead fish may be washed up on the shore.

Clams, mussels, and other shellfish often eat dinoflagellates. They are not harmed, but the poison builds up in their bodies. Anyone who eats contaminated shellfish is in great danger, and can die within a few hours.

THE NIGHTSHADE FAMILY

▲ KILL OR CURE

Foxgloves contain a powerful poison called digitoxin, which acts on muscles in the heart. If a mammal eats a foxglove's leaves, its heart starts to beat more powerfully than usual and its heartbeat slows down. If the animal keeps eating, it risks a heart attack. But, like many plant poisons, digitoxin can also be used as a medicinal drug. It is prescribed to help people suffering from heart failure, but it has to be administered with care – three times the right dose can kill.

▲ PLANT AGAINST PLANT

Plants do not only use poisons to fend off animals. Some kinds, such as this black walnut tree, use poison to stop other plants growing too close. Black walnut roots give off poison and this creates a patch of bare ground around the tree where other plants cannot live. It guarantees space and light for the tree. Black walnuts live in woodland, but this kind of chemical warfare is also common in deserts, where plants need all the water they can get.

Monarch caterpillar has warning colours

Adult monarch butterfly feeds on milkweed nectar

DEADLY NIGHTSHADE
The nightshade family contains hundreds of plants which produce poisons called alkaloids. Alkaloids have important uses as medicines, but in large amounts they can kill. Deadly nightshade berries are rich in an alkaloid called atropine. It speeds up the heart and interferes with the part of the brain that controls breathing.

HENBANE
Normally found on waste ground, henbane has trumpet-shaped flowers with a network of purple veins. This strong-smelling plant produces an alkaloid called hyoscyamine, which affects the central nervous system. Hyoscyamine was once used to sedate people suffering from severe nerve disorders.

AUTUMN MANDRAKE
Since ancient times, people have used the poisons in mandrake to make sleeping draughts and other potions. The plant's forked root sometimes looks like a human body. People thought mandrake screamed when it was dug up, and that the sound could kill. Sometimes they used a dog, tied to the plant, to pull up the root.

THORN APPLE
Also known as jimson weed, the thorn apple is a common wayside weed in the tropics. It contains several poisonous alkaloids, including atropine and scopolamine. Both affect parts of the nervous system that control internal organs, heartbeat, and breathing. Thorn apple gets its name from its spiky seed capsules.

TOBACCO
The main poison in tobacco is nicotine, a highly addictive drug. Nicotine protects tobacco plants by killing insects, and it is sometimes used as a commercial insecticide (chemical to kill insect pests). Wild tobacco comes from Central and South America, but tobacco is now grown as a crop in many parts of the world.

◄ FEEDING ON POISONS
Poisons are not always foolproof, because animals can become immune to them. Milkweed contains powerful heart poisons, but monarch butterfly caterpillars feed on it without coming to any harm. The caterpillars actually store the poisons in their own bodies and use them as a protection against hungry birds, which soon learn that the caterpillars are bad to eat. Adult monarchs also contain the poisons and are protected in the same way.

 Warning: Never touch or eat any plant that you are unsure about because it may be poisonous.

DESERT PLANTS

Deserts are hostile places for plants. Most receive less than 25 cm (10 in) of rain a year. When rain does come, it often falls in torrents that wash away any soil. Deserts can be extremely hot in the day, then freeze at night. Strong winds bombard plants with grit and sand. Plants cope with these conditions in different ways. Some collect enough moisture to survive months or even years of drought. Others, called ephemerals, come to life for a short time after it rains.

◄ SAGUARO CACTUS
Standing up to 17 m (56 ft) high, the saguaro is the world's largest cactus. Like most cacti, it is armed with spines, but it does not have any leaves – instead, it collects sunlight with its enormous, fluted stems. The stems also work like water tanks. When it rains, they slowly expand as they take up water from the ground. Saguaros have creamy-coloured flowers that are pollinated by hummingbirds and bats. They grow slowly, but they can live to be 150 years old.

Fluted sides expand when stem takes up water

Saguaro cactus is the tallest plant in the Sonoran Desert

Desert shrubs often have leaves only in winter and spring

LIVING WITH DROUGHT ►
North America's Sonoran Desert is home to over 2,500 kinds of plant. There are 300 different species of cactus, including the majestic saguaro – a tree-sized giant that can weigh more than 1 tonne (1 ton). Plants are often separated by patches of bare ground, because each one soaks up all the rain that falls nearby. The Sonoran's plant life is particularly rich because it has reliable winter rain. The world's driest deserts are much more barren.

ANATOMY OF A CACTUS

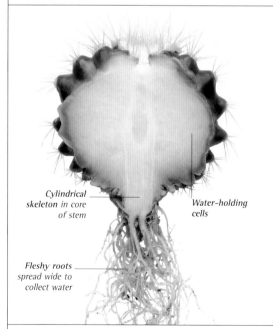

Cylindrical skeleton in core of stem

Water-holding cells

Fleshy roots spread wide to collect water

There are more than 2,000 kinds of cactus, some as big as trees and others no larger than a golf ball. All have the same basic structure, with fleshy, water-holding stems. Most cacti have spines, which are actually modified leaves, as a defence against plant-eating animals. Some have tufts of short, barbed hairs.

Cactus stems carry out photosynthesis. They contain cells that store water and a cylindrical "skeleton" that may remain after the cactus dies and rots. Cactus flowers grow from the top of the stems. Many open at night and are pollinated by bats or moths.

DESERT TREES

QUIVER TREE
Only the hardiest trees can survive in deserts. The quiver tree, from the Namib Desert in southern Africa, stores water in its trunk. Its leaves are small and leathery, so they are less likely to dry out in the sun. The tree gets its name because San people who live in the desert hollow out its branches to make quivers for their arrows.

SACK-OF-POTATOES TREE
The amazing sack-of-potatoes tree grows on the island of Socotra, which is in the Indian Ocean near the entrance to the Red Sea. The tree's fat, sacklike trunk stores water and is topped with several short, stubby branches that put out pink flowers. Socotra has many other unusual plants that are found nowhere else on Earth.

BOOJUM TREE
When it is fully grown, the boojum tree looks like a living pole. It has very short branches that look like bristles, and sometimes much longer ones that resemble arms. Its leaves are tiny, and they fall off during the hottest time of the year. This tree grows only in the Baja California peninsula, in northwest Mexico.

▲ SUCCULENTS
This stonecrop from southern Africa is a succulent – a plant that stores water in its roots, stems, or leaves. Cacti are succulents, too. In a succulent, the water is held in special cells that give the plant a fleshy feel. Succulents often have a waxy covering on their leaves, which helps to stop their water reserves evaporating into the air. If their leaves fall off, they can often take root and become new plants.

SURVIVING HEAT AND COLD ▶
Not all deserts are hot. The Great Basin Desert, in the western United States, is warm in summer and bitterly cold in winter. Most cacti cannot cope with these conditions, because they die if they freeze. The most common plants are low-growing shrubs such as sagebrush. Although it grows slowly, sagebrush covers huge areas. Silvery hairs protect its leaves from the bright sunlight and cold winds.

Teddy bear cholla has spine-covered branches that look fuzzy and furry

DESERT OASES ▶
In many deserts, water is hidden not far beneath the surface. These date palms are growing in an oasis – a place where there is water all year round. Many oasis plants arrive as seeds, blown in on the wind, but date palms are often planted by people as a useful source of food. Some oases are just a few metres across. One of the largest – the Kharga Oasis in Egypt – is over 200 km (124 miles) long.

◄ DESERT IN BLOOM
This teddy bear cholla cactus is surrounded by a colourful carpet of ephemeral flowers. Unlike cacti and desert shrubs, ephemerals have very short life spans. Their seeds lie dormant in the ground until they are brought to life by rain. When this happens, they germinate rapidly and complete their lives in a handful of weeks. By the time the ground dries out again, the adult plants are dead, but they have scattered their seeds.

Desert wild flowers appear after rain

desert plants

MOUNTAIN PLANTS

Life on mountains is harder for plants than life on lower ground. Trees grow on many mountains, but rarely all the way to the top. Plants above the tree line must cope with intense sunshine, strong winds, and bitter night-time cold. High-altitude plants, known as alpines, survive by having small leaves and deep roots, and by staying close to the ground. Some grow at altitudes of 6,500 m (21,300 ft) – where humans find it hard to breathe.

▲ SURVIVAL ABOVE THE SNOW LINE
This dogtooth violet is growing up through a blanket of snow in Russia's Altai Mountains. Snow can be a problem for mountain animals, but it often helps plants to survive. In winter, it forms a protective layer that shields plants from the worst of the cold and wind. In spring, many alpines start growing before the snow melts, so they are ready to flower as soon as it disappears.

ALPINE FLOWERS

SPRING GENTIAN
In early summer, the alpine zone is often filled with plants in flower. The spring gentian is one of the most eye-catching, with sky-blue flowers that attract pollinating bees. There are more than 400 kinds of gentian, and they grow in mountains in temperate parts of the world. Some flower in autumn, rather than spring.

HIMALAYAN PRIMULA
Primulas like cool, damp conditions. Many grow among rocks above the tree line or in mountain pastures. This beautiful species, from the Himalayas, is only about 10 cm (4 in) high. Alpine primulas are often grown by gardeners, too. Many colourful varieties have been produced by interbreeding wild primulas.

AQUILEGIA
Also known as columbines, aquilegias have bell-shaped flowers on upright stems. Each petal has a hollow tube or spur, which contains a pool of nectar at its far end. Aquilegias are pollinated by bumblebees. Using their long tongues, the bees reach into the spurs to drink the nectar and pollinate the flowers at the same time.

◄ LIVING CUSHIONS

Like many mountain plants, this saxifrage has short, closely packed stems, which form a cushioned mound close to the ground. This cushion shape helps to protect the plant from icy winds, and also stops the plant snapping under the weight of heavy snows. Inside the cushion, the temperature can be as much as 10°C (18°F) warmer than the surrounding air. Saxifrage is a Latin name that means "rock-breaker". The plant is so-called because its roots grow deep into crevices in the rock, and look as though they are splitting rocks apart.

◄ ENCRUSTING PLANTS

Instead of forming cushions, scabweed spreads over rocks like a living crust. At an average of 1 cm (½ in) high, it is one of the world's flattest flowering plants. Also known as mat daisy, scabweed comes from New Zealand. Its ground-hugging shape helps it to survive the strongest mountain winds. Lichens (partnerships between algae and fungi) are flatter still, and they grow even higher up. They live on rocks near the summit of Mount Everest and also in Antarctica, on some of the coldest and windiest mountains in the world.

LAYERS OF LIFE

Snow line
Bare rock
Alpine plants
Tree line
Coniferous trees
Broad-leaved trees

Mountain plants change with altitude. In temperate parts of the world, broad-leaved trees grow on the lowest slopes. Higher up, they give way to conifers, which are better at withstanding cold and snow. As the altitude increases, the conifers become smaller and more stunted. They come to a halt at the tree line – above this, conditions are too cold for any trees to grow.

Beyond the tree line is the alpine zone, which is filled with low-growing flowers during spring and summer. If the mountain is high enough, the alpine zone gives way to bare rock and then, above the snow line, to permanent snow. In this icy world, only microorganisms and lichens can survive.

SHIELDED FROM THE SUN ►

On high mountains, the sun is so strong that it can do great damage to leaves. Like many high-altitude plants, this silversword's leaves are protected by silvery hairs, which reflect some of the light that falls on them. Silversword grows only in the Hawaiian islands, on the barren slopes of volcanoes. It lives for up to 20 years, produces a giant cluster of flowers, and then dies.

AFRICAN GIANTS ►

Most alpines are small, but East Africa's mountains are home to some giant plants that are found nowhere else in the world. This giant lobelia on the rocky slopes of Mount Kenya will grow to 3 m (10 ft) or more. It lives on the equator, where the sun is extremely fierce during the day. At sunset, its spiky leaves fold inwards to protect the plant from the night-time cold.

ALTIPLANO PLANTS ►

These mosses are growing in the Altiplano, a high plateau in the Andes mountains of South America. Parts of the plateau are very dry. Rain is rare, and the only reliable moisture comes in spring from melting snow. When this meltwater runs out, mosses become inactive and turn dry, crisp, and grey. Flowering plants, such as cacti, are able to carry on growing because they store water in their roots or stems.

e ►►
mountain plants

FRESHWATER PLANTS

Freshwater is often surrounded by lush vegetation – a sign that it is a prime habitat for plants. Many plants grow at the water's edge, but true water plants live in the water itself. Water plants range from tiny duckweeds to papyrus plants that tower above passing boats. Plant life in freshwater is affected by many things, including the water's depth and the amount of dissolved nutrients that it contains. The more nutrients there are, the faster plants can grow.

◄ LIFE ADRIFT
Instead of growing in one place, frog-bit spends its life drifting on the surface. Its roots trail in the water and its heart-shaped leaves lie flat on the surface. In the autumn, frog-bit makes special winter buds. These sink below the surface before the water freezes over. They float back to the surface in spring, when the ice has thawed. Frog-bit lives in shallow water in Europe, Asia, and North Africa.

Duck spreads duckweed with its feet

THE FRESHWATER WORLD ►
Freshwater habitats vary in size from tiny ponds to wetlands that cover over 10,000 sq km (3,860 sq miles). Shallow lakes are a perfect habitat for water lilies, which root in the mud on the bottom and send up leaves that float on the surface. Most water lilies cannot live in water that is more than 3 m (10 ft) deep.

Duckweed stem floats on surface

◄ DUCKWEEDS
Duckweeds are the world's smallest flowering plants. Each one has a tiny, egg-shaped stem and, usually, one or more roots that trail in the water. The world's smallest duckweed is simpler still, because it has no roots at all. Duckweeds can reproduce by budding off new stems, which float away to take up life on their own. In spring and summer, they can multiply so fast that they cover ditches and ponds with a blanket of green.

Duckweed root hangs down in the water

LIVING UNDERWATER ►
Canadian pondweed spends its life underwater, except when it flowers. This fast-growing plant has small, curly leaves and forms thick tangles in shallow lakes and ponds. Its tiny flowers grow on slender stems that reach upwards until they break through the surface of the water. Pondweeds help to oxygenate (put oxygen into) the water and they give young fish somewhere to hide. They are useful in aquariums, but it is important to pick the right type. Canadian pondweed is so vigorous that it can quickly overrun a small tank.

REED MACE ▶

Easily spotted by its velvety, poker-like flower heads, reed mace grows in shallow ditches, ponds, and lakes. It arrives as wind-borne seeds, but it spreads by means of vigorous underwater rhizomes (horizontal stems). A single rhizome can grow over 2 m (6½ ft) a year, throwing up new plants as it goes. As time goes by, the remains of dead reed mace build up and they help to turn open water into a leafy marsh.

PAPYRUS ▶

In tropical Africa, papyrus forms giant clumps around the edges of lakes and slow-flowing rivers. Papyrus stems are triangular and they can grow nearly 5 m (16 ft) high. Each one is topped by a ball-shaped flower head that has dozens of stiff, green spokes. In the distant past, papyrus was a plant with many uses. The ancient Egyptians used it to make cloth, matting, and ropes, as well as one of the earliest forms of paper.

SWAMP CYPRESS ▶

Most trees find it hard to grow in water, because their roots cannot collect the oxygen they need. The swamp (or bald) cypress gets around this problem by having special growths on its roots called "knees". These stick out above the surface and collect oxygen from the air. The swamp cypress is a conifer but, unlike most of its relatives, it loses its leaves in the winter. It grows in Florida's Everglades and other parts of southeast USA.

Leaf pad of the Amazon water lily turns up at the rim

e ▶▶ freshwater plants

◀ FLOATING GIANT

The Amazon water lily, from South America, has the largest floating leaves in the world. Each one is up to 2 m (6½ ft) across, with a vertical rim around the edge. A notch in the rim allows rainwater to drain away. The leaves contain lots of air spaces that keep them afloat and they have a network of spiny ribs underneath. This structure makes the leaves remarkably strong: when fully grown, they can support the weight of a child lying down.

COASTAL PLANTS

On coasts, plants have to withstand strong winds and salty spray. It is a tough combination, particularly when it is made worse by hot sunshine or severe winter cold. On rocky coasts, most plants grow close to the ground, so that they keep out of the wind's way. On low-lying coasts, plants face different problems because their home is never still. Shingle is shifted by the waves, sand is blown by the wind, and mud is moved by the tide. Plants that grow here often have deep roots, and special ways of getting rid of surplus sea salt.

coastal plants

THE SEASHORE WORLD ▶
The coast is like many habitats in one. Lichens live on bare rock – black kinds closest to the sea itself, with bright orange ones growing higher up. Above them, salt-tolerant plants grow in cliff crevices that are soaked by salty spray. Cliff-top turf is a good place for seeing wild flowers, which grow beyond the reach of the waves. Rocky coasts are also home to coastal shrubs, which can cope with onshore winds.

◀ CLIFF PLANTS
With its rounded shape and bright pink flowers, thrift is one of the most colourful plants found on rocky shores. Also known as a sea pink, thrift grows in rocky crevices just beyond the reach of the waves. Thrift leaves are slender and leathery, and the plant's beautiful flowers are not as delicate as they look. They have strong stems and tough petals, and can easily survive gale-force winds. Thrift grows throughout the northern hemisphere, on mountains as well as on the coast.

COASTAL SHRUBS

MAQUIS
The shrubby vegetation found on rocky ground around the Mediterranean Sea is known as maquis. It contains evergreen shrubs and low-growing trees. Many maquis plants have a strong, aromatic smell, which comes from oil stored in their leaves. These oils stop leaves from drying out during the hot Mediterranean summer.

BANKSIAS
In southern Australia, shrubs called banksias grow close to the shore. Banksias have tough, evergreen leaves and candle-shaped flower heads that contain hundreds of flowers. Banksias flower for months at a time. They give the birds that pollinate them a year-round supply of food as well as somewhere to nest.

FYNBOS
The evergreen vegetation that grows on South Africa's Cape coast, as well as its inland mountains, is known as fynbos. The name means "narrow-leaved" and its shrubs cope with hot summers and strong winds. Fynbos contains an amazing variety of plants and is one of the botanical hotspots of the world.

◄ GROWING ON SAND

Close to the shore, sand dunes are constantly reshaped by the wind. Only a few plants can survive here. One of the most widespread is marram grass (see page 51), which helps to hold the sand in place. Further inland, dunes do not move so much and their sand contains fertile humus (rotted-down plant remains). These more permanent dunes are home to a wider variety of coastal plants, including orchids, sea holly, and even small trees. Pines often grow on inland dunes. They thrive on the poor, sandy soil, and their leaves can cope with strong sea breezes.

◄ GROWING ON SHINGLE

Shingle is the toughest habitat for coastal plants, because the small stones are easily rolled around by the waves. Worse still, shingle cannot hold water, so any rain runs straight through it. The sea pea is one of the few plants that can survive in shingle, thanks to its extra-long roots and its unusually tough leaves and stems. Its seeds look like small, black peas and have a hard outer coat that stops them being cracked open during storms. They can survive for up to five years in sea water, which helps the sea pea to spread to new shingle banks.

SALT MARSHES ►

Salt marshes form on low-lying coasts, where rivers carry sediment to the shore. The tide creates a muddy landscape riddled with channels and creeks. The driest parts of a salt marsh are often covered with grasses, sea lavender, and other salt-tolerant plants. Sea lavender is named for its purple flowers, which bloom in late summer. Its long roots reach deep into the mud and keep the plant anchored at high tide.

MUD FLATS ►

Glassworts grow all around the world on flat, muddy shores. Also known as marsh samphire, these unusual plants are less than 15 cm (6 in) high. They have fleshy stems and small, scalelike leaves. In spring, glassworts are bright green, but by the summer they have often turned deep red. Glassworts contain lots of salt and were once used to provide soda for glass-making. Some are collected and pickled for eating.

OCEAN TRAVELLERS

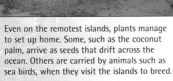

Even on the remotest islands, plants manage to set up home. Some, such as the coconut palm, arrive as seeds that drift across the ocean. Others are carried by animals such as sea birds, when they visit the islands to breed.

Plants also travel with human help, when people deliberately or accidentally spread them to new places. Sometimes introduced plants can be a problem, because they compete with plants that are already there.

MANGROVE SWAMPS ►

Flat, muddy coastlines in the tropics are home to mangrove trees – the only trees that can survive in saltwater. Mangroves have tough, evergreen leaves and arching prop roots (support roots that grow out from the stem and reach deep into the mud). Some mangroves have special breathing roots that stick out of the mud and collect oxygen from the air. Mangrove swamps are very important habitats for wildlife.

FOOD PLANTS

Early humans hunted animals and gathered wild plants. Then, about 10,000 years ago, people learned to grow plants for food. Farming transformed the way people live and changed the face of the world. Today, we depend on cultivated food plants to survive. Cereals are the most important. We also grow hundreds of different kinds of fruit and vegetables, and plants that give us herbs, spices, and edible oils.

◄ OIL CROPS
Olives are one of the world's oldest oil-producing crops. Originally from around the Mediterranean, they have been grown for at least 5,000 years. Other oil crops include oil palms, groundnuts, sunflowers, and colza (oil-seed rape). As well as providing us with a high-energy food, some plant oils are also used to make detergents, soap, and paints.

Olive turns black as it ripens, but can be eaten green

Farm worker picks the olives by hand or shakes the tree so they fall

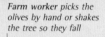

MAIZE: 721 MILLION TONNES

WHEAT: 627 MILLION TONNES

RICE: 605 MILLION TONNES

 BARLEY: 153 MILLION TONNES

 SORGHUM: 59 MILLION TONNES

▲ CEREALS
This chart shows the world's yearly harvest of cereals or grain. Cereals are packed with energy-rich starch, useful dietary fibre, and vitamins. Just three cereals – maize, wheat, and rice – make up half of the plant food that humans eat. Maize and wheat grow mainly in temperate parts of the world, such as North America, Europe, and southwestern Australia. Rice grows in the tropics, in flooded fields called paddies.

FARMING METHODS

SUBSISTENCE FARMING
People who carry out subsistence farming grow just enough to feed themselves and their families. Each farmer works a small plot of land. He or she often raises a number of different crops and also rears farm animals. Subsistence farming is hard work, but the costs are low because farmers use little or no machinery.

INTENSIVE FARMING
On an intensive farm, crops are grown on a massive scale and machinery takes the place of human labour. As a result, a small team of workers can grow more food than thousands of people working by hand. Intensive farmers also use a wide range of chemicals to kill weeds and pests, and to fertilize the soil.

▲ LEGUMES

A legume is any food plant that belongs to the pea family. Legumes include dozens of kinds of peas and beans, and they are cultivated all over the world. One of the first legumes to be grown was the lentil – a pea-like plant from the Middle East. Legume seeds are easy to store and they are a good source of protein. Legume plants help to fertilize the soil, because their roots contain bacteria that turn nitrogen from the air into nitrates that improve the soil.

food plants

◄ FRUIT PLANTS

As well as tasting good, fruit is an important source of vitamins. Hundreds of different fruits are grown. Some, such as oranges, are farmed on a huge scale and eaten all over the world. Others, such as these durians, are local specialities. Durians come from southeast Asia. They are prized for their taste, but they have such a powerful smell that they are often banned on buses and trains.

Durian weighs up to 4 kg (9 lb) and has spiny skin

Edible pulp surrounds the durian's seeds

◄ VEGETABLES

People eat many different plant parts as vegetables – the leaves of cabbage, the flower heads of broccoli, and the buds of Brussels sprouts. Vegetables also include plant stems, such as celery and asparagus, and plant roots such as carrots. Cucumbers and aubergines are not classed as vegetables. They contain seeds and are actually types of fruit.

Long stem often sprawls over the ground

Leafy shoots can be used as animal feed

Sweet potato's skin may be red, purple, or white

HERBS AND SPICES ►

For thousands of years, people have used herbs and spices to flavour their food. Herbs are grown all over the world and consist mainly of leaves. Spices come largely from the tropics and include many different plant parts. Turmeric powder is made by grinding up turmeric roots, while cloves are the flower buds of a small, evergreen tree. Pepper, the world's most popular spice, is made from the dried berries of a climbing vine.

Turmeric has a distinctive dark yellow colour

Chilli powder is made from pulverized, dried chilli peppers

▲ ROOT CROPS

Many plants store food in their roots, which is why root crops are useful sources of energy. In the tropics, people grow sweet potatoes, cassava or manioc, taro, and yams. However, the world's most important root crop is the potato. More than 300 million tonnes (295 million tons) of potatoes are grown each year and there are thousands of varieties. Sweet potatoes and true potatoes are not close relatives, but they both grow edible tubers underground.

PLANT BREEDING

Most of the food plants we eat today are very different from their wild relatives. This is because farmers have improved crops through selective breeding. To do this, a farmer sows seeds from the best plants. The result – over many years – is a crop that produces more food. Farmers have used selective breeding since prehistoric times, but today a completely new technique is also used in plant breeding. Genetic modification, or GM, enables scientists to insert useful genes directly into crop plants.

◄ MAIZE

Maize comes from Central America, where it has been cultivated for at least 6,000 years. Its wild ancestor is a grass called teosinte, which has tiny cobs (or ears) that fall apart when they are ripe. Through selective breeding, farmers transformed this unpromising plant into a cereal that is now grown worldwide. Unlike teosinte, maize does not scatter its grains, so it cannot grow without human help.

Teosinte is the wild ancestor of maize

Maize cob contains hundreds of kernels

Potatoes may be small with irregular shapes

Skin colour range from bluish-black to light yellow

▲ GENETIC VARIATION

This Peruvian woman is selling potatoes, which originally came from the high plains, or Altiplano, of South America. People have grown potatoes here for at least 7,000 years, and they raise many varieties that are unknown in the outside world. These local varieties are of great interest to plant breeders, because they sometimes contain beneficial genes that can be bred into modern crops. Genes like these can be useful in fighting off plant diseases and animal pests.

WHEAT AND ITS ANCESTORS

WILD EINKORN
This wild grass from the Middle East is one of the ancestors of cultivated wheat. Before people learned to farm, they collected its seeds as food. Wild einkorn has small grains that drop off the plant when they are ripe. Around 9,000 years ago, people began to cultivate einkorn, selecting plants to produce larger grains.

WILD EMMER
Found in Egypt and the Middle East, this wild grass is the ancestor of emmer – one of the earliest kinds of wheat. Wild emmer has larger grains than wild einkorn, with long, spiky bristles called awns. Cultivated emmer was once an important crop, but it was eventually replaced by hybrid wheats such as spelt.

SPELT WHEAT
This form of wheat appeared in Europe about 3,000 years ago, when einkorn and emmer hybridized, or interbred. Spelt wheat has large grains, and they stay attached to the plant when they are ripe, which makes them easier to harvest. Until the 20th century, spelt wheat was one of the world's most important crop plants.

MODERN WHEAT
Thanks to scientific plant breeding, modern wheat is more productive than any of its ancestors. This bread wheat contains high levels of gluten. The proteins in gluten make dough elastic, so that it can rise. Another modern wheat, durum wheat, contains less gluten and is used for foods such as pasta and biscuits.

▲ ARTIFICIAL POLLINATION

This farmer is pollinating vanilla flowers so they will produce a good crop of pods. Artificial pollination is routine with crops such as pumpkins and custard apples, because their natural pollination rate is low. It can also be used to produce hybrids, by taking pollen from a different variety of plant. Hybrids are often stronger than either of their parents, which is why they make good crops. Many food plants, from wheat to grapefruit, have been produced in this way.

▲ EASIER HARVESTS

As well as making yields bigger, plant breeding can make crops easier to harvest. These apple trees have been grafted (joined) onto special rootstocks (the stumps and roots of another variety of apple tree). This keeps their trunks short and means that the fruit is easier to reach. Plant breeders have also produced dwarf cereal plants with shorter and stronger stems. Unlike taller cereal varieties, these ones are less likely to get flattened during storms.

▲ THE GREEN REVOLUTION

Armed with a spray gun, this Chinese rice farmer is treating his fields against crop pests. The rice that he is growing was developed in the 1970s, during a worldwide crop-breeding programme called the Green Revolution. This research effort produced new strains of rice that yield three times as much grain as traditional varieties. The drawback with these "miracle" crops is that they often needs lots of artificial fertilizers and pesticides to thrive.

HOW GENETIC MODIFICATION WORKS

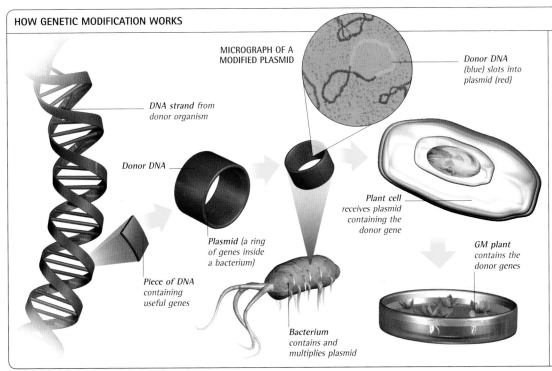

MICROGRAPH OF A
MODIFIED PLASMID

*Donor DNA
(blue) slots into
plasmid (red)*

*DNA strand from
donor organism*

Donor DNA

*Plasmid (a ring
of genes inside
a bacterium)*

*Piece of DNA
containing
useful genes*

*Bacterium
contains and
multiplies plasmid*

*Plant cell
receives plasmid
containing the
donor gene*

*GM plant
contains the
donor genes*

Genes are chemical instructions that are carried by all living things. In genetic modification, scientists identify useful genes and move them from one living thing to another. They cut the genes from their strands of DNA using chemicals called restriction enzymes. Then they insert the genes into bacteria, which copy them many times. Finally, the bacteria containing the copied genes are inserted into the plant.

Genetic modification is often used with crops, because it is quick and precise. It can make crop plants grow faster and it can help them fight off pests and diseases. Genetic modification can also reduce waste, by making fruit and vegetables last longer after they have been harvested.

◄ GM CROPS AND THE ENVIRONMENT

These demonstrators are tearing up a field of genetically modified oil-seed rape. They want to stop GM crops being grown, because they believe the crops' genes could escape into wild plants: windborne GM pollen might fertilize wild plants and produce hybrids, for example. Anti-GM protests have been widespread in western Europe, but in North America, GM crops are already grown on a large scale. Scientists are divided about GM technology. Some think it could solve the world's food shortages. Others are concerned about the long-term effects of genetic modification.

breeding

PRODUCTS FROM PLANTS

Apart from food, plants provide us with thousands of products that are important in everyday life. Houses and furniture contain timber from trees, while wood pulp is the main ingredient in paper and cardboard. Plants also provide us with natural fibres such as cotton and flax, which are used to make fabrics and clothing. Plant-based ingredients are used in perfumes and cosmetics, as well as in many industrial products, such as polishes, varnishes, printing inks, and paints. In addition, sugars from plants can be turned into ethanol, which is a low-pollution fuel.

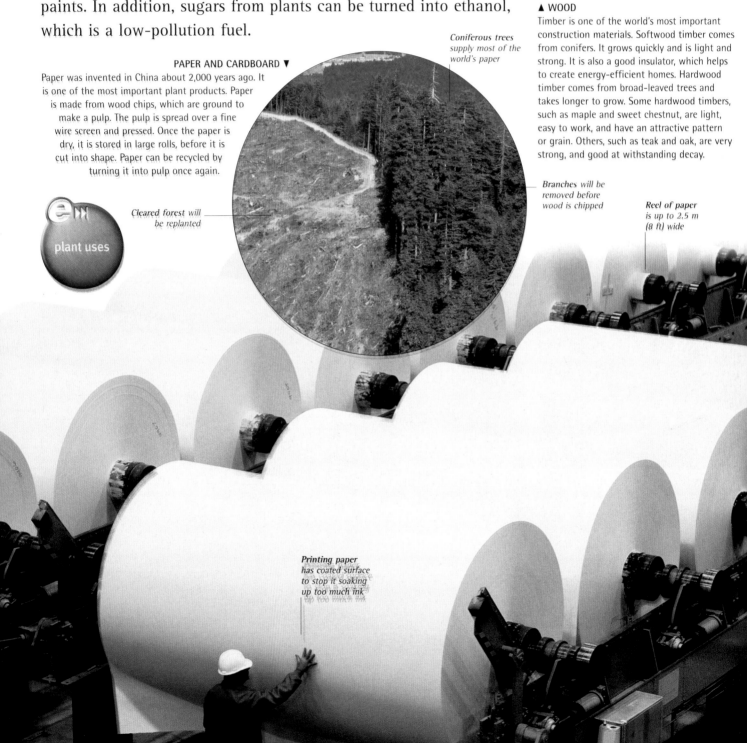

▲ WOOD
Timber is one of the world's most important construction materials. Softwood timber comes from conifers. It grows quickly and is light and strong. It is also a good insulator, which helps to create energy-efficient homes. Hardwood timber comes from broad-leaved trees and takes longer to grow. Some hardwood timbers, such as maple and sweet chestnut, are light, easy to work, and have an attractive pattern or grain. Others, such as teak and oak, are very strong, and good at withstanding decay.

PAPER AND CARDBOARD ▼
Paper was invented in China about 2,000 years ago. It is one of the most important plant products. Paper is made from wood chips, which are ground to make a pulp. The pulp is spread over a fine wire screen and pressed. Once the paper is dry, it is stored in large rolls, before it is cut into shape. Paper can be recycled by turning it into pulp once again.

Coniferous trees supply most of the world's paper

Branches will be removed before wood is chipped

Reel of paper is up to 2.5 m (8 ft) wide

Cleared forest will be replanted

plant uses

Printing paper has coated surface to stop it soaking up too much ink

PLANT FIBRES ►

Cotton, flax, and hemp are grown for their fibres. Cotton fibres grow in fluffy masses called bolls, which contain the plant's seeds. Bolls are harvested by machine and then their seeds are ginned (combed out), leaving the cotton fibres. The fibres are spun together to make yarn, which is woven to make cotton fabric. Cotton is a good material for making clothes, because it is comfortable to wear and easy to bleach or dye.

RIPE COTTON BOLL

Harvested cotton bolls ready for ginning (seed removal)

PLANT DYES ►

For thousands of years, people have used plants to dye clothes, food, or their own hair and skin. This seed pod, from the annatto tree, produces a bright red dye that is used to colour fabrics and foods.
It originally comes from Central and South America, where native peoples still use it as a body paint. Other important plant-based dyes include indigo, which is dark blue, and henna, which is reddish-brown.

PERFUMES

LAVENDER

This aromatic shrub with blue flowers has been used in perfumes since ancient times. It is cultivated in Europe and North America. Fragrant lavender oil is extracted by pressing its stems, leaves, and flowers, which are covered in oil-containing glands. Lavender flowers are also dried and used to fill sweet-smelling pouches.

GARDENIA

Gardenias are tropical shrubs that grow in Africa and Asia. They have large, white flowers with a very strong, fragrant scent. Many of them are pollinated by moths, which use the scent to find the flowers after dark. Gardenia fragrance is made by collecting the flowers, and then pressing them to extract their oil.

BERGAMOT ORANGE

Unlike other citrus fruits, the bergamot orange has tough, dry flesh. It is cultivated for its sweet-smelling oil, rather than as a food. Oil of bergamot is extracted from the orange peel. It is used in perfumes, including eau de Cologne, and in Earl Grey tea. Bergamot oranges are grown in southern Italy.

SANDALWOOD

This low-growing tree is prized for the aromatic oil that is extracted from its wood. Sandalwood oil is used in perfumes, incense, and traditional medicines. Sandalwood itself has been used to make furniture with a distinctive scent. It grows in Southern and Eastern Asia, but in some areas, it has become rare through over-use.

YLANG-YLANG

Some of the world's most famous perfumes (including Chanel No.5) are made with the oil from the ylang-ylang tree, which grows in Southeast Asia. Ylang-ylang oil is extracted from the tree's flowers, which grow all year round. The oil is expensive, because it takes about 1 kg (2¼ lb) of flowers to produce just 10 drops of oil.

▲ PLANT OILS

As well as edible oils, plants produce oils that are used in other ways. Palm oil and olive oil are both used to make soap because they are mild on the skin. Castor oil is used to make a variety of industrial products, from brake fluid to printing ink, while linseed oil is used in varnishes and artists' oil paints. Plant oils are normally liquid, but many can be turned into solids by a process called hydrogenation. Margarine is made by hydrogenation.

▲ PLANT-BASED FUELS

In some parts of the world, such as Brazil, sugar cane is used to produce vehicle fuel. Sugary sap is extracted from the cane and then fermented by adding yeast. The yeast turns the sugar into ethanol – a liquid alcohol that engines can burn. Ethanol-based fuel is less polluting than petrol, because it contains less sulphur. It can also free countries from dependence on imported mineral oil, which will continue to become more expensive as reserves run short.

medicinal
plants

MEDICINAL PLANTS

Long before the start of modern medicine, people knew that plants could help to fight disease. Some of the world's earliest books were herbals – books that described what medicinal plants looked like and how they could be used. In these days of modern medicine, many illnesses are treated by purpose-made drugs. Even so, four-fifths of the medicines we use are based on plant products or on substances that were originally found in plants. Every year, researchers discover new medicinal plants, and new uses for plants that are already known.

Spike on the edge of the leaf deters animals

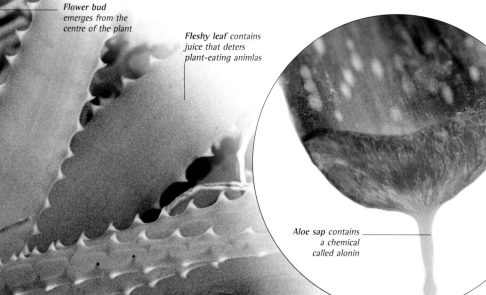

Opium poppy has large flower and waxy leaves

Unripe seed head contains milky sap that is harvested

Flower bud emerges from the centre of the plant

Fleshy leaf contains juice that deters plant-eating animlas

Aloe sap contains a chemical called alonin

◄ PAINKILLERS
For over 5,000 years, opium poppies have been grown for the painkilling drugs found in their milky sap. These drugs include codeine and morphine (one of the most powerful painkillers known). At one time, medicines containing opium were used to treat diarrhoea and to help people sleep, even though they can have dangerous side effects. Today, opium poppies are still grown to produce medicines, but they are also farmed illegally, to produce the drug heroin.

▲ PROMOTING HEALING
Since ancient times, people have used plants to treat bites and stings, and to heal wounds and bruises. Aloe vera, the juicy sap from the *Aloe vera* plant, reduces inflammation and soothes burns. It is also used in cosmetics and insect repellents. There are over 200 kinds of aloe, and many have traditional uses as medicines. Originally from tropical Africa, aloes are now cultivated in many other parts of the world.

ANTI-ASTHMATICS ►
Ephedras are evergreen shrubs that produce a drug called ephedrine, which opens up the airways to the lungs. The ancient Chinese took it to treat asthma and hay fever. Today, ephedrine is made synthetically, instead of being extracted from plants. After it is inhaled, ephedrine works very gradually, but a single dose can be effective for several hours.

ANTI-MALARIALS ►
Malaria is a dangerous disease that affects about 250 million people a year. The bark of the cinchona tree has been used to treat malaria for about 300 years. It contains quinine, a drug that stops malaria parasites reproducing in an infected person's blood. Quinine is difficult to make, so most of it still comes from cinchona trees.

ANTI-CANCER DRUGS ►
Like most yew trees, the Pacific yew is poisonous. However, it is also a source of taxol, an important cancer-fighting drug. Taxol interferes with cell division, so it makes it harder for cancerous cells to grow and spread. The rosy periwinkle is another plant that contains cancer-fighting drugs. It is used to treat leukaemia and Hodgkin's disease.

TRANQUILLIZERS ►
Many medicinal plants have an effect on the nervous system. For hundreds of years, the powdered roots of a woody shrub called rauvolfia have been used as a tranquillizer and to reduce blood pressure. The plant's active ingredient, reserpine, was the first drug to be successful in treating mental illness. It is no longer prescribed because it has unwanted side effects if it is taken for a long time.

Rauvolfia flower is tubular, with red stalks and white petals

Leaf is leathery and evergreen

Coca leaves are processed to make cocaine

DRUG MISUSE ►
After intercepting a suspect ship, these customs officers are inspecting a haul of illegal drugs. Many drugs from plants are secretly refined and sold. The main sources are cannabis, opium poppies, and coca (a South American shrub that is used to produce cocaine). Illegal drugs can be harmful to health and they fuel crime. However, despite international efforts, the trade in drugs has proved very difficult to control.

HERBAL REMEDIES

CONEFLOWER
Also known by its scientific name, echinacea, this plant comes from the prairies of North America. It can be used to heal wounds, but it is also thought to boost the immune system (the part of the body that fights infections). Coneflower was one of the most important plant remedies used by American Indians.

EVENING PRIMROSE
Evening primrose is a relatively new herbal remedy, first used in the 1970s. Evening primrose oil contains fatty acids and is believed to improve the circulation and to help treat the symptoms of arthritis. Evening primrose originally comes from North America, but it is cultivated in many other parts of the world.

MAIDENHAIR TREE
The ginkgo, or maidenhair tree, has fan-shaped leaves that contain high levels of antioxidants – substances that help to preserve the complex chemicals inside living cells. Many herbalists believe that extracts from ginkgo leaves can help to keep the body healthy and also slow down the effects of ageing.

ASIAN GINSENG
Meaning "root of heaven" in Chinese, ginseng is one of the most famous herbal remedies. For centuries, its roots have been used in the Far East as a tonic – something that improves general health and keeps disease at bay. A closely related plant grows in North America and seems to have the same beneficial effects.

COMMON VALERIAN
Also known as allheal, valerian is a traditional remedy for insomnia (sleeplessness). Unlike synthetic drugs, it helps people to sleep without producing unpleasant side effects. It is also used to lower blood pressure and reduce stress. Valerian extract is prepared from the plant's roots, which are dried and then crushed.

WEEDS

A weed is any plant that grows where it is not wanted. Weeds are a problem for gardeners and farmers because they compete with cultivated plants for space, water, and light. They can also help pests and diseases to spread to garden plants and crops. Weeds can be even more troublesome if they are carried beyond their normal home, because they can become invasive and crowd out local plants. Weeds are controlled in three different ways: by digging them up, by treating them with chemicals, or by using their natural enemies.

Dandelion flower produced almost all year round

Tough leaf can withstand trampling

Long taproot resprouts if it snaps near the top

Seed head relies on the wind to spread seeds

Root

◄ ANATOMY OF A WEED
The common dandelion is one of the world's most successful weeds. Originally from Europe and northern Asia, it has been accidentally spread to many other regions, from North America to Australia. Dandelions are tough, so they can survive being trodden on, and they have deep taproots which are hard to dig up. They are not harmed by frost or by dry weather, and they spread far and wide using seeds that float away on parachutes of fine hairs.

HOW WEEDS SPREAD ►
The butterfly bush or buddleia originally came from China, but it is now a common weed in many other parts of the world. In the 1800s, it was brought to Europe and North America as a garden plant, but it managed to escape. It thrives on waste ground, in gravelly places, and along railway lines. If its roots can collect enough water, it even manages to survive high up on bridges and walls. In summer, the bush's purple flowers produce lots of sweet-smelling nectar, which attracts butterflies from far and wide. Some butterflies can smell a single buddleia from over 1 km (½ mile) away.

▲ GARDEN WEEDS
For gardeners around the world, weeding is an essential task. Most garden weeds are annual plants, which germinate as soon as the soil is dug. Chickweed, groundsel, and other annuals usually have shallow roots, and are easy to pull up. Perennial weeds, such as dandelions, are more of a problem. Their roots reach deeper into the soil, and they often resprout if they are snapped off. To stop perennials regrowing, every part of the plant has to be removed.

▲ FARMLAND WEEDS
In farmland, different weeds grow in different kinds of fields. These horses are grazing in pasture – a favourite habitat of stinging nettles, thistles, docks, and other perennial weeds. Farm animals eat grass and soft-leaved plants, but they leave the weeds alone. As a result, the weeds slowly spread. In arable (crop-growing) fields, most weeds are annual plants. These weeds often germinate before the crop starts to grow, and harvesting helps to spread their seeds.

▲ WATER WEEDS
Some of the world's worst weeds live in freshwater. This picture shows a floating plant called water hyacinth. It originally came from South America, but it has been accidentally spread throughout the tropics, where it lives on rivers, lakes, and ponds. Water hyacinth grows very rapidly, shading out water wildlife, and making it hard for fish to survive. It clogs the propellers of boats and can even stop turbines working in hydroelectric dams.

Worker cuts back invading scrub

King protea is South Africa's national flower

▲ FIGHTING ALIEN PLANTS

Armed with a machete, this conservation worker in South Africa is helping to beat back invading plants. Funded by the Worldwide Fund for Nature (WWF), this work is designed to protect the fynbos, a type of vegetation found nowhere else in the world. Fynbos has an amazing variety of native plants, including aloes, pelargoniums, and proteas, but many of them are threatened by alien plants that have invaded their habitat. Many of these plant invaders are Australian shrubs and trees, which were introduced into South Africa over a century ago.

CACTUS MOTH

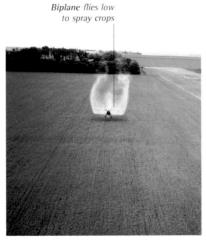

Biplane flies low to spray crops

▲ BIOLOGICAL WEED CONTROL

During the 1920s, prickly pear cacti from South America ran wild in eastern Australia. Within a few years, over 15 million ha (37 million acres) of farmland were covered with cactus plants. To deal with the menace, scientists brought in a South American moth that feeds on the cactus. Within five years, it stopped the invader in its tracks. This method of fighting weeds is called biological control.

▲ CHEMICAL WEED CONTROL

Swooping over a field, this plane is spraying a crop with a herbicide (weedkiller). Some herbicides kill all plants, but the one being used here is selective, which means that it kills the weeds, but not the crop. Herbicides have revolutionized farming and helped farmers to grow much more food. But herbicides have some drawbacks. They harm wildlife and are sometimes dangerous to human health.

INTRODUCED INVADERS

BLACK WATTLE
This fast-growing tree originally comes from Australia, and it lives in places with poor, dry soil. One of the reasons why it has been introduced to other parts of the world is because it is a good source of firewood. It also contains nitrogen-fixing bacteria in its roots, so it helps to fertilize the soil. In southern Africa, black wattle has become a problem, because it uses up water that local plants need to grow.

JAPANESE KNOTWEED
A perennial plant that forms large clumps, Japanese knotweed was introduced to Europe and North America as a garden plant. Unfortunately, it soon escaped and is now found in waste places and along road sides, particularly where the soil is damp. It crowds out other plants, and its dead stems form dense thickets that take a long time to die down. It is difficult to kill, even with strong herbicides (weedkillers).

KUDZU VINE
Also known as mile-a-minute vine, this vigorous climber comes from China and Japan. It can grow 10 m (33 ft) a year, and it sprawls over the ground and up trees. Introduced in North America as a garden plant, it has become a major plant pest, and now infests over 2 million ha (5 million acres) of land. In many states, planting it is illegal. Fortunately, it cannot withstand severe frost, so this has limited its spread.

LANTANA
This low-growing, tropical shrub has neat leaves and aromatic orange or red flowers. Despite its attractive appearance, lantana is an unwelcome sight in many warm parts of the world. It often takes hold in pastures, because cattle do not eat its rough leaves and woody stems, and its berries are poisonous. However, lantana cannot tolerate frost, so it can be safely grown as a garden plant in places where the winter is cold.

PURPLE LOOSESTRIFE
A common wildflower from Europe, purple loosestrife grows on river banks and in freshwater wetlands. In its natural home, other plants keep it in check, but in North America it often runs out of control and crowds out native plants. Purple loosestrife is good at spreading. Just one loosestrife stalk produces as many as 300,000 seeds. The plant also has creeping stems, or stolons, which help it to form large clumps.

STUDYING PLANTS

Botany (the study of plants) is one of the oldest sciences. Over 2,000 years ago, in ancient Greece and China, expert herbalists collected plants and described their use as medicines. In the 1700s, the Swedish botanist Linnaeus invented a system of naming plants that is still used today. Since then, botanists have learned a vast amount about how plants work. Modern botanists work in laboratories, botanical gardens, and natural plant habitats all over the globe. Botany is important because the world is changing rapidly. Plant habitats are shrinking, and botanists are working hard to save plants under threat.

botany

THE SEARCH FOR NEW SPECIES ▶
Using a hand-held lens, a botanist investigates a pitcher plant in the rainforest of southeast Asia. After a close look at the living plant, he will take samples of its leaves and flowers, so that it can be identified. If it turns out to be a new species, it will be described in detail and then given a scientific name. This work helps to safeguard rare plants, because recognizing them is the first step towards protecting them. Botanists have been studying plants for centuries, but they still have lots to learn. Hundreds of new species are discovered every year – not only in remote rainforests, but also in urban areas.

Plant specimen has been pressed and preserved

▲ PRESERVING PLANTS
This drawer contains a single pressed plant, laid out on a paper sheet. Pressing gently squeezes the moisture out of a plant, but preserves all the details of its shape. Because the specimen is dry, it can be stored indefinitely without rotting away. A collection of pressed specimens is called a herbarium. One of the world's largest, at Kew Gardens in London, contains over five million specimens, and the collection grows bigger and bigger every year.

HABITAT DESTRUCTION ▶
This rainforest in southeast Asia is being cleared by farmers desperate for land. Trees are also cut down for their timber. When rainforest trees disappear, so do other forest plants, such as orchids, palms, and ferns. According to the International Union for the Conservation of Nature (IUCN), over 8,000 of the world's plants are currently endangered.

PLANT CONSERVATION ▶
Tissue culture is a technique that can save endangered species. Some of a plant's cells are removed, then groups of cells are placed in test tubes, on a layer of nutrient gel. After several weeks, each group becomes a new plant, complete with roots and leaves. Tissue culture cuts out the work of pollinating flowers and waiting for seeds to grow.

SEED BANKS ▶
Across the world, special seed banks store seeds from endangered species. Unlike living plants, seeds can be stored for decades or even centuries. In the future, these seeds can be used to re-establish plants in the wild. Seed banks also store seeds from old varieties of crops, to stop them disappearing completely as new varieties are brought in.

▲ BOTANIC GARDENS
These desert plants are growing in the Princess of Wales Conservatory at Kew Gardens, one of the world's leading centres for plant research. Botanic gardens are places where scientists study plants, and where visitors have a chance to see plants and enjoy them in climate-controlled glasshouses. Modern botanic gardens often raise plants that are rare and endangered in the wild.

COUNT LOUIS-ANTOINE DE BOUGAINVILLE

Bougainvillea flowers are surrounded by colourful, leafy bracts

▲ PLANT NAMES
When a new plant is identified, it is given a scientific name. This often describes features of the plant, but it can also commemorate the person who first collected it. For example, the eye-catching climbing plant *Bougainvillea glabra* is named after Louis-Antoine de Bougainville, a French naval officer who explored the islands of the South Pacific. The second word, *glabra*, is Latin for "smooth" and describes the plant's hairless leaves.

ENDANGERED SPECIES

CUCUMBER TREE
This rare tree grows on the island of Socotra, off the Horn of Africa. It is the only tree in the cucumber family, and it has a water-storing trunk that helps it to withstand drought. During droughts, farmers often feed its watery flesh to their animals, which is why it is becoming rare.

ALERCE
The alerce is a large conifer that comes from rain-soaked mountainsides in southern Chile and Argentina. From the early 1600s, European settlers exploited it for its timber, and today only a fraction of the original alerce forest remains. The tree is now protected, but illegal logging continues.

ST HELENA BOXWOOD
This small shrub lives on the remote island of St Helena in the southern Atlantic. There are fewer than 20 wild plants left. Habitat loss and damage from livestock are the main threats. However, botanists have been collecting boxwood seeds and hope to re-establish the plant in the wild.

GOLDEN PAGODA
Like many South African shrubs, the golden pagoda is threatened by non-native plants that are invading its habitat. Fortunately, the golden pagoda is popular with gardeners all over the world. The plant lives on in cultivation, even though it has become rare in the wild.

MANDRINETTE HIBISCUS
This plant lives only on the island of Mauritius in the Indian Ocean. Alien plants have taken over its habitat, so few plants survive in the wild. The mandrinette faces another problem: it interbreeds with the common hibiscus, so purebred mandrinette plants are becoming increasingly rare.

PLANT CLASSIFICATION

Non-flowering plants

SPORE-PRODUCING PLANTS

Division	Common Name	Families	Species	Distribution	Key Features
HEPATOPHYTA	Liverworts	69	8,000	Worldwide	The world's simplest plants, without true roots, stems, or leaves (although some kinds have leaflike flaps). Low-growing, and restricted to damp habitats, they reproduce by scattering spores.
ANTHOCEROPHYTA	Hornworts	3	100	Mainly tropical and sub-tropical regions	Simple plants that resemble liverworts, but which may have evolved separately, from green algae. Hornworts live in damp places, and get their name from their hornlike, spore-bearing structures.
BRYOPHYTA	Mosses	92	9,000	Worldwide, but most common in temperate regions	Diverse, simple plants that often have a cushion-like or feathery shape. Their spores develop inside capsules that grow on slender stalks. They live in damp woodlands, peat bogs, and on bare rock.
PSILOPHYTA	Whisk ferns	1	6	Tropical and sub-tropical regions	The simplest vascular plants (ones with internal pipelines that carry water). Their spore-producing stage has a whisk-like shape, with finely divided branches. Whisk ferns may grow on other plants.
LYCOPHYTA	Club mosses	3	1,000	Worldwide	Low-growing plants that have true roots, creeping or upright stems, and small, scalelike leaves. They often grow on forest floors. Club mosses were the dominant plants in the Coal Age (354–290 mya).
SPHENOPHYTA	Horsetails	2	15	Worldwide	Brushlike plants that have cylindrical stems, whorls of narrow leaves, and separate, spore-producing stems. They are common in damp places, such as the banks of streams, and often form clumps..
PTEROPHYTA	Ferns	27	11,000	Worldwide but most common in tropical regions	Plants with well-developed roots, fibrous stems, and complex leaves. Most grow on the ground; some grow in freshwater or on other plants. They make up the largest group of non-flowering plants.

GYMNOSPERMS *Non-flowering seed plants*

Division	Common Name	Families	Species	Distribution	Key Features
CONIFEROPHYTA	Conifers	7	550	Worldwide but most common in the far north	Non-flowering, wind-pollinated plants that have woody stems and that produce seeds in female cones. Most are trees, but some are low-growing shrubs, and almost all have evergreen leaves. Their leaves and wood often contain aromatic resin.
CYCADOPHYTA	Cycads	4	140	Mainly tropical regions	Palmlike plants with thick, woody stems and a crown of compound leaves. Cycads are either male or female. Female cycads produce seeds inside cones, while male ones shed pollen. Most cycads are wind-pollinated, but some are insect-pollinated.
GINKGOPHYTA	Ginkgo	1	1	Originally from China and Japan; now cultivated worldwide	A single species of tree (also known as the maidenhair tree) with distinctive, fan-shaped leaves. Each tree is either male or female; female ones produce fleshy-coated seeds, which look like yellow berries when they are ripe.
GNETOPHYTA	Gnetophytes	3	70	Mainly tropical and sub-tropical regions	Diverse, non-flowering seed plants that often live in deserts and dry places. They include densely branched shrubs called ephedras, and welwitschia, which grows only in the Namib Desert. Gnetophytes may be wind- or insect-pollinated.

ANGIOSPERMS *Flowering plants* Division ANTHOPHYTA

Class MAGNOLIOPSIDA *Plants with two seed leaves (dicots)*

Subclass	Common Name	Families	Species	Distribution	Key Features
Magnoliidae	Magnolias and relatives	39	12,000	Worldwide	Plants that have simple flowers (rather than flower heads), with sepals and petals often arranged in a spiral. They include both woody and soft-stemmed plants, such as magnolias, water lilies, buttercups, and poppies. They are the most primitive dicots.
Hamamelidae	Witch hazels and relatives	24	3,400	Worldwide	Plants that typically have small, wind-pollinated flowers, often arranged in catkins. This group includes some soft-stemmed plants, such as nettles and hemp, but also many trees and shrubs, such as witch hazel, planes, birches, beeches, and oaks.
Caryophyllidae	Pinks and relatives	13	11,000	Worldwide	Plants that are usually soft-stemmed and often have colourful flowers. Most are low-growing, and some are common weeds. They include pinks and carnations, sugar beet, spinach, and climbers such as bougainvillea. Cacti also belong to this group.
Dilleniidae	Cotton and relatives	78	25,000	Worldwide but most common in tropical regions	Plants that usually have simple (undivided) leaves, and sometimes flowers with petals that are joined. They include many trees and shrubs, and many crop plants, such as papaya, squashes (pumpkins, marrows, and cucumbers), cotton, cacao, and tea.
Rosidae	Roses and relatives	116	60,000	Worldwide	Plants that have flowers with separate petals and numerous stamens. They include several of the world's largest plant families, such as peas, spurges, and the rose family itself, as well as rafflesia (the plant with the largest flower).
Asteridae	Daisies and relatives	49	60,000	Worldwide	Plants that often have joined petals, with stamens attached to the inside. They include many major plant families, including the mint and potato families. In the daisy family, plants have compound flowers, made of many florets packed together.

Class LILIOPSIDA *Plants with one seed leaf (monocots)*

Subclass	Common Name	Families	Species	Distribution	Key Features
Alismatidae	Pondweeds and relatives	16	400	Worldwide	Plants that are soft-stemmed and that grow in water or on the surface. They include marsh arrowgrass, freshwater pondweeds, and also eelgrasses, which grow in the sea. They are the most primitive monocots.
Commelinidae	Grasses and relatives	16	15,000	Worldwide	Plants that generally have small flowers that are pollinated by the wind. They include grasses (one of the most widespread and successful families of flowering plants), rushes, reeds, sedges, and bromeliads. Most are soft-stemmed.
Arecidae	Palms and relatives	6	4,800	Worldwide but most common in tropical regions	Plants with small flowers, arranged in groups, that are clasped by a leafy flap called a spathe. They include palms (about 2,800 species), aroids (such as the Swiss cheese plant), and duckweeds (the smallest flowering plants).
Liliidae	Lilies and relatives	19	30,000	Worldwide	Plants that are typically soft-stemmed, with narrow leaves, and eye-catching flowers. As well as lilies, they include irises, daffodils, agaves, yams, and orchids (one of the largest families of flowering plants). They are the most advanced monocots.

GLOSSARY

Algae A varied group of simple, plantlike organisms that make their food by photosynthesis. Most algae live in water.

Alien plant A non-native plant that has escaped into the wild.

Alkaloid A type of chemical produced by some plants that can affect animals' bodies. Alkaloids include stimulants, such as caffeine, and poisons, such as strychnine.

Alpine plant A plant that grows on bare mountainsides above the tree line. Most alpines are low-growing and cushion-shaped.

Angiosperm A flowering plant that reproduces by making seeds. The seeds grow inside a protective chamber called an ovary, which ripens to form a fruit.

Annual A plant that completes its life cycle in a single growing season (one year).

Anther A male part of a flower that makes and releases pollen.

Asexual reproduction Any kind of reproduction that does not involve male and female cells. For example, a plant may grow a stem or bud that eventually becomes a new, separate plant.

Bacteria Single-celled microorganisms that are the simplest and most abundant living things on Earth. Some bacteria cause plant diseases; others live in partnership with plants, and help them to collect nutrients from the soil.

Biennial A plant that takes two years to complete its life cycle. It flowers, fruits, and dies in its second year.

Biological control A way of controlling pests and diseases that uses their natural enemies, instead of synthetic chemicals.

Botany The scientific study of plants.

Broad-leaved tree Any tree that is a flowering plant, rather than a conifer. Broad-leaved trees may be evergreen or deciduous.

Bulb Underground plant part that stores food. A bulb is formed from swollen leaf bases or from fleshy scales wrapped around each other.

Carpel The female part of a flower, made up of a stigma, which collects pollen, and an ovary, where the seeds develop. The two are linked by a stalk called a style.

Cell A tiny unit of living matter, wrapped in an ultra-thin membrane. In plant cells, the outer membrane is surrounded by a tough wall. Most plants contain different types of cell, shaped to do different tasks.

Cellulose A building material that is made by plants. Plants use cellulose to build cell walls.

Cell wall A fibrous jacket around a plant cell, made from cellulose. Cell walls work like scaffolding, giving plants the support that they need to grow.

Cereal A cultivated grass, such as wheat or maize, which is grown for its edible grain.

Chlorophyll The green pigment (coloured chemical) that plants and algae use to absorb energy from sunlight to use in photosynthesis.

Chloroplast A microscopic structure that contains chlorophyll. Chloroplasts use chlorophyll to collect energy from sunlight.

Chromosomes Microscopic structures found in most living cells. Chromosomes contain chemical instructions, called genes, that build living things and make them work.

Clone A collection of plants, or other living things, that have been produced by the same parent, using asexual reproduction. Cloned plants share exactly the same genes.

Composite flower A flower head made up of many miniature flowers, or florets, packed together. The result looks like a single flower.

Compound leaf A leaf that is divided into separate parts, or leaflets, which are attached to the same stalk.

Conifer A non-flowering tree or shrub that grows its seeds in cones, and that usually has evergreen leaves. Conifers are not the only coniferous (cone-bearing) plants, but they are by far the most numerous and widespread.

Coniferous plant A non-flowering plant that produces seeds in cones. Most coniferous plants are evergreen trees.

Cotyledon A small leaf that is packed inside a seed. Some cotyledons store food, and never open up like normal leaves. Others open up quickly when a seed germinates, collecting energy so that the seedling can grow.

Deciduous tree A tree that loses all its leaves for part of the year.

Diatom A microscopic, single-celled alga that has a case made of silica. Diatoms teem in the surface waters of the oceans, where they soak up the energy in sunshine.

Dicot A flowering plant that has two cotyledons (seed leaves).

Dioecious Having male and female flowers on separate plants.

DNA Short for deoxyribonucleic acid. DNA is the substance that living things use to store information. It works like a chemical recipe, building cells and controlling how they work. *See also* chromosomes

Dormant Inactive for a long period of time. Seeds remain dormant so that they can survive difficult conditions.

Embryo A young, undeveloped plant, packed away inside a seed.

Ephemeral plant A plant that germinates, flowers, and sets seed in a very short period of time. Most ephemerals live in dry places, and come to life soon after it rains.

Epidermis The outermost layer of cells in a plant's leaves, stems, or roots.

Epiphyll A plant that grows on another plant's leaves, where it can soak up sunlight.

Epiphyte A plant that grows on other plants, particularly trees, but that does not steal their food or nutrients (unlike a parasitic plant).

Evergreen tree A tree that has leaves all year round.

Evolution A slow change in plants – and all living things – that allows them to adapt to their environment over many generations.

Fertilization The moment when a male cell joins a female cell to produce a new individual. In flowering plants, fertilization happens after pollen has been transferred from one flower to another. Once it has occurred, a flower can start to make seeds.

Filament In a flower, the stalk that supports an anther, so that it can scatter its pollen.

Floret A miniature flower that forms part of a composite flower.

Flower head A cluster of flowers that grows from a single stem.

Fossil The remains of living things that have been preserved in rock. Plant fossils help botanists to see how plants have evolved.

Fruit A ripened ovary that contains seeds. Flowering plants use fruits to help spread seeds.

Gametophyte In a simple plant, such as a liverwort or fern, the stage in the life cycle that produces gametes (sex cells). *See also* sporophyte

Genes Chemical instructions that control the way living things grow, and the way they work. Genes are made from DNA, and they are copied and passed on when living things reproduce.

Genetic modification (GM) A way of artificially transferring useful genes from one kind of living thing to another. For example, GM is used in crop plants to increase their yields.

Germination The start of growth in a seed or a spore, often triggered by moisture and warmth.

Glucose A sugar that plants make by photosynthesis. Glucose provides the energy that plants need to grow.

Growth regulator A chemical that affects how quickly a plant's cells divide, usually speeding up the process, but sometimes slowing it down.

Growth ring One of the rings that can be seen in tree trunks when they are cut down. Each ring is a layer of wood grown in a single year. The total number of rings shows a tree's age.

Gymnosperm A plant that reproduces by making seeds, but which does not have flowers or fruit; the seeds usually form inside cones.

Habitat A particular environment where a plant (or any other living thing) lives.

Halophyte A plant that can live in salty habitats, such as coasts or near salt lakes.

Hemiparasitic plant A plant that steals some of its water and nutrients from other plants.

Hydrophyte A plant that lives in water.

Kingdom In scientific classification, the largest category of living things. Most biologists divide the living world into five kingdoms: animals, plants, fungi, protists, and bacteria. Protists include algae, the living things that are the closest relatives to plants.

Latex White, unpleasant-tasting sap made by some plants to ward off plant-eating animals.

Legume (1) A plant that belongs to the pea family. (2) A seed pod that splits when it is ripe.

Liana A large, woody-stemmed climber that is particularly common in tropical rainforests.

Lichen A living partnership between a fungus and microscopic algae. Lichens often grow on bare rocks, and other extreme habitats where plants cannot survive.

Midrib The large, central vein that runs down the middle of a leaf.

Monocot A flowering plant that has one cotyledon (seed leaf).

Monoecious Having separate male and female flowers on the same plant. Maize is an example of a monoecious plant.

Node The part of a plant's stem that bears one or more leaves.

Ovary In flowering plants, the part of a flower that contains developing seeds.

Ovule In flowering plants, a tiny cluster of female cells that develops into a seed. Before the seed can form, the ovule has to be fertilized by male cells from pollen grains.

Parasitic plant A plant that steals all the food and water that it needs from another plant, known as its host. Unlike most plants, parasitic plants do not have working leaves.

Perennial plant A plant that lives for several years. All trees and shrubs are perennials, and so are many soft-stemmed plants that die down to ground level during the winter.

Petal A leafy flap on a flower. It is often brightly coloured to attract pollinating animals.

Phloem A network of cells that work like pipelines, carrying food that a plant makes by photosynthesis to all the parts of the plant.

Photosynthesis The way that plants and algae make their own food: they contain a pigment called chlorophyll that reacts with sunlight, carbon dioxide, and water to make glucose.

Phytoplankton Tiny organisms that float in water, and that live like plants by collecting the energy in sunlight.

Plankton Small or microscopic living things that spend all or part of their lives in water.

Pollen Dust-like particles that contain a flower's male sex cells.

Pollination The transfer of pollen from male parts of a flower to female parts, so fertilization can occur and seeds can develop. Pollen may be tranferred by animals or the wind.

Radicle An embryo root inside a seed.

Rhizome A creeping, underground stem that some plants use to spread.

Root hair A microscopic growth near the tip of a root that absorbs water and nutrients from the soil.

Runner A stem that spreads horizontally over the ground, producing new plants as it grows.

Sap The fluid that carries water, nutrients, and dissolved food to different parts of a plant. Sap flows through microscopic pipelines called xylem and phloem cells.

Seed bank A collection of seeds that have been gathered, dried, and put in long-term storage.

Seed leaf *See* cotyledon

Selective breeding A way of improving plants by collecting seeds from parent plants that have useful or attractive characteristics.

Sepal A leafy flap that protects a developing flower. Unlike petals, sepals are often green.

Sex cell A male or female cell that is used in sexual reproduction. In flowering plants, male cells are in pollen and female cells are in ovules.

Sexual reproduction Reproduction that involves one male and one female parent. Unlike asexual reproduction, it produces varied offspring – for example, plants with different coloured flowers.

Simple leaf A leaf that is not divided into separate parts.

Species The basic unit that scientists use in classifying living things. The members of a species look similar and can interbreed with each other in the wild.

Spore A tiny package of cells, or a single cell, that can germinate and develop. Simple plants and fungi use spores to spread.

Sporophyte In a simple plant, such as a liverwort, moss, or fern, the stage in the life cycle that produces spores.
See also gametophyte

Stamen A collection of male parts in a flower. Each stamen has an anther, which makes pollen, and a filament, which connects the anther to the rest of the flower.

Starch An energy-rich substance that plants use as a food store. Starch is an important ingredient in many staple human foods, such as wheat, rice, and potatoes.

Stigma A female part of a flower that collects incoming pollen grains.

Style In a flower, the stalk that connects a stigma to an ovary.

Succulent Any plant that survives in dry places by storing water in its roots, stems, or leaves.

Taproot A plant's main root, which usually has smaller roots branching off it.

Tendril Threadlike leaf grown by some climbing plants. Tendrils coil around nearby objects and help plants to hold onto supports as they climb.

Testa A ripe seed's tough, protective coat.

Transpiration The loss of water vapour through pores in the leaves. This process helps to draw up more water from the roots. Water supplies useful minerals, keeps plant cells firm, and is also used in photosynthesis.

Tuber A swollen, underground stem that stores food, or helps a plant to spread. Potatoes are examples of tubers.

Weed Any plant that is growing where it is not wanted.

Xerophyte A plant that is specially adapted for life in dry conditions.

Xylem A network of cells that work like pipelines, carrying water from a plant's roots to its leaves.

INDEX

A page number in **bold** refers to the main entry for that subject.

ACKNOWLEDGEMENTS

Dorling Kindersley would like to thank Lynn Bresler for proof-reading and the index; Christine Heilman for Americanization; and Dr. Olle Pellmyr for her yucca moth expertise.

Picture Credits

The publisher would like to thank the following for their kind permission to reproduce their photographs:

Abbreviations key:

t-top, b-bottom, r-right, l-left, c-centre, a-above, f-far